What makes you YOU?

Discover the hidden forces
that shaped your Being,
and how to choose
your Becoming.

Jon Freeman

For Yannis

Published by: SpiralWorld

www.spiralworld.net

ISBN 978–0993-3192-8-0 Paperback

ISBN 978–0993-3192-9-7 Digital

Spiral World

Contents

Introduction: When Consciousness Becomes Form

For every atom belonging to me as good belongs to you

Walt Whitman – "Song of myself" in Leaves of Grass

What makes you YOU?

I wonder what comes to your mind as you see the title question. I can see several likely answers.

- You might think of yourself as a product of your environment and upbringing. "I am who I am because of my parents, family, community and education.

- You might think of experiences you have had –events that formed you – which could include both positive experiences with specific influencers and negative or unsupportive ones. It could include the political events that made you a refugee or the death of a parent when you were young.

- You might think of your genetics and view yourself as predestined to be the way you are.

This book explores these themes and many more that might be less obvious or familiar. Some of them might be quite new to you or even seem strange until you see how it all weaves together.

The majority of what I will describe has been part of my direct experience. I have spent decades exploring and the more aspects I have encountered, the more wonderful the richness of life they have revealed. More than that, the more I have learned, the more see there is still to discover. I am not unique. Everything that I point to here is also true of you. Humans are truly extraordinary and magnificent. Whatever your self-image might be, whatever doubts, pains or fears you have, and however you see your life, that is the reality[1] of existence. If you don't see this now I hope that by the end of this book you will - and feel both better for it and more empowered to choose what's next.

What makes me, me?

How do I come to be the person writing this? I couldn't have foreseen this when I was 20 or 30. No one else would have either. Some of the reasons might have been visible in my nature, that I am stubbornly curious. I have always needed to know how the world works. Some of them might be seen in my father, who always believed that life should be better than it is and, in his way, worked to make it so. I learned that attitude and behaviour. My mother was a professional musician, such that I was immersed in something intangible and non-visible, which speaks to us from beyond intellect, through emotion, connection and direct appreciation. Music remains a passion, often in the background as I write.

I can point to events too. I was at university in the 1970s, a time of dope and LSD. I had my mind opened and its boundaries stretched. A decade later, during a training, I had a significant, evidenced psychic experience which contradicted the fundamentals of my scientific education. The stubborn curiosity I referred to above kicked in, big-time. I don't see that stopping. Meanwhile, it produced the worldview behind this book, blending science and spirituality, and framing the relationship that you and I have with our worlds[2]. It made me a practical mystic.

---

[1] I use the word "reality" a lot in this text. In most instances it denotes a worldview, what we perceive to be real. There is another meaning which may sometimes apply. My SD colleague Ben Levi defines that one as "that which exists, even when I stop believing in it".

[2] Those who are instantly curious about the science might like to read my book "The Science of Possibility: Patterns of Connected Consciousness". It's on Amazon, Kindle and most of the other places you might expect to find it.

Genetics is something else. Like many others I have had my genetic origins mapped and I know where I come from, the mix of countries my ancestors have passed through. But only in a limited sense is that who I am because I have also learned that the explanation we have been given about genes was a long way from the truth. They are not an immutable blueprint. That tale is not who I am because genes and their expressions are not fixed. The real story is much more exciting.

When Consciousness Becomes Form

The overarching frame of this book is the story of what happens when consciousness becomes form. More particularly, what happens when the form is human, and when that human is you?

The essence is simple, but it is also multilayered, because there are many aspects to who you are, probably more than you are aware of. The book is a journey through those layers for you to discover more about the uniqueness of your Being. It is also an exploration of what that leads to, of how we live. Who can you Become, how do you choose that, and how does that also create what is best for all humans and for life on Earth? The path may be unfamiliar, though it arrives at conclusions about the importance of love, care, kindness and mutuality that you will easily recognise. It endorses both human spirit and divine spirituality in a fresh and intentionally practical way, by telling a radically new story about how we reclaim that space of love and connection. What if love is, and always has been, the ultimate strategy?

The unfamiliarity arises from a new way to view our existence. The idea that consciousness becomes form is the opposite of what most of us have been taught to think. The conventional presentation is that consciousness is something inside of you, something that your brain creates and your mind perceives. That presentation is profoundly false and deeply damaging, both individually and collectively. It separates us. It is at the root of the gulf between material and spiritual approaches to life. You cannot live in flow when you can't even acknowledge its existence. You cannot find coherence when your world is fundamentally fragmented.

What happens when we start to see this the right way round? It is hardly a new concept to suggest that there is oneness and connection across all of creation; our challenge has been to embody that reality and live accordingly. This book provides two key conceptual threads that link the elements. They help you reorient yourself, see the flow and connect with it, supporting you to navigate accordingly.

How does consciousness become form? The answer will reveal a field that informs the shapes that energy takes when it becomes matter, in the same way that a magnet's field causes iron filings to form patterns. This **Information Field** provides a dynamic and flexible structure to the Universe, and it does the same for this book, because it lives within and connects every layer of who you are. The Information Field is the container for the flow, the shape of the riverbank. You have always been connected with it and embedded in it. By becoming more aware of what it has to say, you can literally become more informed, and shape your life accordingly.

Since the Information Field connects everything to everything else, it is also a place of relationships. We are not a collection of objects in a billiard-ball universe. We are living, experiencing and being. We are flows of activity and awareness and choice, none of which is in isolation, all operating in the places of connection to other flows. Those other flows may look like other people, or other life forms, or even other entities in our world such as companies and neighbourhoods. We label them as if they are objects too, but they are all areas of relationship. Consequently, our world is a place of **Relational Being**. As the book unfolds, it will show how this way of viewing life expands the possibilities of what you can do and the life you can create.

The essence of this book

All that is personal to you sits within that big frame, and the way that its new perspectives lead to fresh ways to think, be, and choose your life. Genetics, environment and events are just a few of the shapers that have moulded you. You may have noticed from my example that all three are involved, and perhaps you noticed other responses coming to your mind. How many more might there be?

I won't offer a number, because there are too many overlaps. This should not be surprising, since you are one single being in whom many different elements are functioning together. Listing every component would quickly become absurd. Your spleen and your liver are both significant and an acupuncturist might see them separately. We can't go to that level of detail, and I hope that you will find it comforting that we won't break down the picture to every pixel. Some aspects of existence, although relevant, may only be mentioned in passing, sometimes pointing to references for further exploration.

Thus, I am trying to focus on what is essential to this story, which is for you to encounter more fully the richness of who you are and then what that makes possible for your future. That second aspect will be our endpoint because the purpose of the book is to support development and expansion. Individually, this can include how you approach your own personal growth; collectively, it extends into a shift in our perception of how the world operates. That is because the YOU question cannot be separated from the US question and the UNIVERSE question. Our focus is not directly on the deep philosophical issues of what life is and why we even exist at all. That might show up indirectly though, because seeing ourselves in a new way brings in a new frame for reality.

We will achieve that by reflecting the whole in a personal mirror. The way that breaks down is approximately as follows.

- ❖ There is a history to who you are from before your conscious awareness. There are fields of information that affect you – fields in the family and ancestry and other influences that I will call cosmological. There are also experiences in utero, at birth and during infancy that shape you in ways that you would not be aware of. The results show up in your body as well as your thinking.

❖ We are each raised immersed in a miasma of mindsets – cultural, religious, family and "tribe" belief systems, religious contexts, and early socialisation. You are affected by place and time. All of these begin when you are young, some before you are verbal, and more as you start to develop your identity. They become components of who you are, with varying degrees of subtlety. You may know the expression "you can take the girl out of the hills, but you can't take the hills out of the girl". There is so much more to that truism than is generally recognised.

❖ As we get a little older we learn more consciously. Our schooling teaches us specific ways to think and be. Our training and deeper socialisation come from many other people, from the media, from what we learn about the contexts of politics, economics, and science. These influence what we believe to be "reality", and they cut us off from many aspects of it. Who you are is very heavily shaped by all of this, and changing it requires asking tough questions about what is actually true.

The above leads into the territory of our relationships with the world around us. When we are cut off there are consequences, not in all cases but in many. We don't see other people in their fullness or connect with them emotionally as we might. We can't connect with the dynamics of the natural world. We don't recognise or trust our intuition. Our view of anything that might be called "spiritual" is greatly diminished. Many of us have been bruised by religious dogma and doctrine, and we haven't been taught how to have a direct connection to anything in that non-material realm. On the contrary - we are taught to be sceptical.

We have been led to believe that faith is the ability to mentally accept something irrational and magical, and therefore not real. We are told to trust the authority of those who supposedly know better (or have more faith). We are trained to doubt and distrust our instincts. Our culture does not teach us how to recognize our own knowing, how to experience our connectedness, or how to have faith in either. You may be like many I know who have rejected religion and consider that personal faith and experience should be possible, but don't know how to access them.

The inability to relate to more than a few aspects of what is around us, beyond us, and within us pushes us back to a limited version of ourselves. This restricts us to closed-off self-sufficiency or to an unconnected inner consciousness which has no relationship to the natural world. We are then deprived of the spiritual nourishment that could be available from either the cosmos or Earth. Many feel obliged to settle for the next best option, which is human community and human spirit. That is not a bad choice, but we could have that and so much more. Meanwhile, lack of spiritual connection reduces our awareness, resulting in options based on more limited input. As you will come to see, choices are paramount.

We will end our journey there by joining up the alternatives that are available to us, many of which will have shown up on the road. What holds us back, and how can we remove those blocks? What has made us unsafe and how do we find a place of security and confidence to be who we are? What can we do to connect more and better? How do these aspects show up in our development and what moves us towards greater individual and collective health and balance? By the close, I aim for you to feel more empowered, more able to change, having an increased awareness of flow and an expanded sense of what is possible for you to do.

There's a lot to explore. Let's take our first step.

Discovering the Field

"I must assume behind this force the existence of a conscious and intelligent mind. This mind is the matrix of all matter".

Max Planck (German theoretical physicist whose discovery of energy quanta won him the Nobel Prize in Physics in 1918.)

Where does connection happen?

Let's get into the fundamentals of how this different reality works. If you can grasp a sense of what I am about to describe, what comes later will fall into place more easily.

I'd like to begin with the story of what led me here. The pivotal moment occurred during a training where I had the experience of knowing something I could only have known psychically.

Here's the scenario. I was in a group of three people, one of whom held a card from which she shared three pieces of information about an individual whom she didn't personally know. In that instance, David, a male living in Devon, UK. My task, using techniques we had been taught over three days, was to detect the illness that David was affected by.

In the background I should say that I was raised as a rationalist and atheist, was scientifically trained and had no belief whatsoever in my ability to succeed. For ten minutes or so I was proving that expectation brilliantly, completely blank, whatever technique I used.

Then the third person in the group, who was there to remind me of the tools, suggested that I try the "space helmet technique". What this meant was visualising that I had put David's head over my own in order to feel his reality. So, eyes closed, I imagined and mimed that action.

The effect was dramatic. I instantly had a sensation at the back of my head, left side. I tilted my head and screwed up the left side of my face as if in pain. The words came from my mouth without conscious thought: "Does he have a brain tumour?" I was told that this was what the card said.

Why am I telling you this?

This is not really about me – certainly not in the sense of some special ability. Some others on the training were also detecting information about their subject individuals. But it is about what it caused in my world, and where it has led over the four decades since.

My reality back then was full of scientific knowledge. I knew enough about physics and biology to recognise that what I had done was impossible in conventional terms. And yet it had happened in a quite visceral and undeniable way. No blinding lights, no voice from the heavens; you might say that it was almost mundane. At another level it was quite the opposite, a jaw-dropping experience, a bolt of lightning through my relationship with the world, and quite irreversible. What I had been taught was evidently not the whole truth. It cracked my worldview.

Of course, science still works. My phone does the same things that yours can do and there are satellites orbiting the earth so that I could share a video call with you tomorrow. At the same time, scientific knowledge has an apparent gap. I would like to share what I have learned about that gap, because it is fundamental; it's as if we have a wonderful map, but are holding it upside-down, or squinting through the paper from the other side.

What should the map look like?

An obvious question follows - what does the map look like from the right side? The answer is surprisingly simple, but no less challenging for that. It demands that we see ourselves and the world very differently.

The normal view – the one that we are taught in school, the one that runs through philosophy, physics, medicine and psychology – sees reality as material. Even though humans have spiritual or emotional experiences, atoms and cells are taken to be at the centre. Quantum theory and relativity operate on the fringes of that material-centred view, but even though we know that matter is formed from energy and that quantum-level events are inherently uncertain, the results are presented to us inside a frame of material outcomes.

None of that materialist viewpoint adequately explains the world as it really is. This leads to many of the effects that we don't want, from ecosystems damage and climate change to economic fragility and socio-political challenges. And it certainly falls short of the ability to describe human spiritual experience, often consigning it to a kind of reject pile of faulty brain function. That model of the world has no way to deal with psychic experience in any form. It would reject my story as either a delusion or an outright lie. If that is your view, unless you are curious about where I am going, reading any further will be pointless.

The alternative view places matter in second place. This is consistent with relativity in that it recognises that all matter is formed from energy. But $E=MC^2$ only tells us about quantities of energy and matter. It doesn't tell us about form and shape, nor about how they behave and why they change. What informs (or in-forms) that?

"The stuff of the world is mind-stuff." Arthur Eddington, 1917

What's in first place?

Information. In-form-ation. That is to say, there is something which governs and describes the shapes that energy takes when it becomes matter. That something has continuity. It becomes retained knowledge. It begins at the most basic level of sub-atomic particles. It continues to govern and hold the memory of everything that follows, from the formation of atoms and molecules to biological entities. It is present in all that exists and around all that exists. Omnipresent, you might say.

I can justify those statements in terms of all other scientific understanding. I have done so in depth and at length. But here and for now, I ask you to just accept it and see where it leads and what that implies for who we are, our place in creation, and how massively we might benefit from that understanding.

Our entire relationship with the universe shifts when we grasp the implications. This is not a human-centric perspective though; it's quite the opposite and works just as well without us. The relationship of everything in the universe with everything else also alters because nothing is outside of the connectedness. Everything exists and functions in connection to everything else. It may be familiar to many that there is talk of "oneness" as a potential human experience. However the usual presentation of that has been for it to be viewed as a psychological phenomenon, something that takes place in human consciousness, maybe because such experiences have often been accessed through meditation, shamanistic drumming or psychedelic substances. That makes them seem like a special state.

In contrast, a fully connected universe, independent of human experiencing, presents us with a oneness that is not dependent on us. We are not special. All this existed before humans evolved. The philosophical question of whether the universe continues to exist when I am no longer there to see it was always somewhat foolish and self-centred. When the tree falls in the forest, the sound it makes is witnessed by the forest, and the mycorrhiza experience the change. The universe does not depend on us in any way at all. Get over it!

Where are we headed?

As we explore the features of our being as described in the introduction, many features of the field will reveal themselves. Along the way we will:-

- unpack how it affects human choices both personally and collectively

- look at what it means for our biology, our physiological and our mental health

- open questions of how we move away from a fixed and over-deterministic view of genetics

- see how it shapes our families and inhabits our identity

- encounter the implications for our societal systems, such as our ways with money

- change how we view our relationship with place and with the non-human natural world

- show how it has affected evolution and development

- open into the nature of activity and creative co-creation that becomes possible when we engage dynamically and relationally with the flow of the Information Field

- present implications which empower us in new ways to live, bringing connectedness into our daily existence. Oneness is not a mystical experience but a place from which to live.

The overarching effect of the materialist view that dominates Western society has been that we regard ourselves and others as things. What if you were to think of yourself as a verb rather than a noun? What fresh perspective and living dynamics will that enable? What if we saw Being as something that we are as well as something that we do?

The psychic experience I just described is a single drop in the ocean of what becomes possible when we live into connectedness. Even so, it points the way very clearly. It could only have happened because that information was available and detectable. It could not have happened unless I could locate that information in time and space. As much as it can look like magic, or some kind of miracle, it isn't that at all. Instead, it points towards a form of unrecognised and largely unused technology. It is the universe's open-source operating system and we have access to the code.

Our next chapter will be our first illustration – the first app for us to look at – a very different take on your family history than anything you will find on ancestry.com.

Intrigued? I hope so.

Echoes of the past

"When the family has been brought into its natural order, the individual can leave it behind him while still feeling the strength of his family supporting him. Only when the connection to his family is acknowledged, and the person's responsibility seen clearly and then distributed, can the individual feel unburdened and go about his personal affairs without anything from the past weighing him down or holding him back."

Bert Hellinger

Let's dive straight into something that graphically illustrates one way that the Information Field works, how much more connection we have with it than most of us know, and which has some powerful implications for your identity. This chapter is about family constellations. What follows comes from Juliana Freeman, a trained facilitator and coach who also has deep experience in many aspects of working with the field[3].

What are constellations?

> "Everything seen and everything unseen exists in the field, and we tend to think that only what we see is present and active. But everything's in the field, whether it's seen or not. And so all of the strings that we have, all the connection points we have to our ancestry, to our place in the land, never get seen or expressed unless we open up the field to experience what it is we're not allowing or seeing or acknowledging.
>
> Constellations were originally set up for family systems, though anything can be set up as a constellation in order to see what is

---

[3] Juliana was also co-creator of "The Science of Possibility" and some of her background and stories are described there. She works as a coach and facilitator supporting individuals to expand their awareness of how multiple aspects of hidden history and spiritual connection are affecting their lives, and making new choices possible. To learn more, please see the Other Contributors topic in the Resources section.

unseen. They also work for organisations and societal issues.[4] They reveal what is behind the veil of what we currently see. So, with the constellation you set up a situation where people are asked to represent elements in the field - usually other people - but might also represent other things.

Let's take a family constellation to illustrate this. Somebody would come with a situation, an issue they might want to delve into, perhaps a life situation that's causing them a problem in some area, like depression or anorexia. You set up a representative for them, and then for whoever else or whatever else you glean from the initial interview would be part of that constellation. For example, that might be mother, father, any siblings.

The representatives are entering the field with a completely blank slate, so they have no knowledge of the mother for example, or her circumstances. They are literally walking into a field of energy that the original intention or request from the issue holder, the client, has invoked. They're not trying to figure anything out. They're entering the field intuitively to _be_ the father, to _be_ the mother or whoever, and just to notice what it is they feel. How are their bodies? Where do they feel any sensations?

They are also intuitively placed in the space, usually by the client, but maybe by the client's representative or the facilitator. How do they feel about the position they're in and where they are facing? And then they're asked to just follow their knowing, follow what guides them, to perhaps move from one side of the room to the other; they might adopt a particular stance such as grumpy or maybe angry or sad. They might crumple to the floor. They might lie down.

In one case I saw somebody enter a field to represent a woman's grandfather. Immediately they picked up their leg and stood on one leg. We then later discovered that the grandfather had that part of his leg blown off in the war. But nobody besides the

---

[4] See the book "Invisible Dynamics" in the resources list.

client knows that. And this is an example of what can happen in the field, that people start to take on a different persona than their own. They can then express how they're feeling, how they feel about the others around them in the constellation, such as "I don't like him and want to be as far away from him as possible."

The client would be sitting out with the facilitator, watching this play out. So slowly, by asking each of the representatives, 'how are you here? How is it for you?' you begin to build a picture of what's possibly going on. And then the facilitator might get an intuition or a sense that other people need to come in. For example, if everybody's looking at the ground, he might ask, "What are you looking at?" And they might say, "Well, I'm not sure, but there's something down there." So then a representative is brought in to lie on the ground. Or somebody might be looking outside, just staring out of the field. If somebody is constantly reaching outside of the field you might want to ask for a representative for whatever is outside.

Then you're asking for feedback from these new representatives, like the one on the ground. What is happening here? How are you feeling? They might say, well, I'm not feeling anything at all. The most obvious thing that would be representing is somebody who's died. Quite often, somebody has died and it hasn't been acknowledged, or it hasn't been processed, or that person's death hasn't been fully integrated into the family system. For example, it might be a situation where a child died and the grief was so intense the parents couldn't handle it, and so they carried on as normal, trying to cover everything up. But obviously when you do that, as we will see in the example of the women that were locked away and who couldn't express, when something's not acknowledged or expressed, the field will retain and hold on to that energy until it is.

That plays out through life, so if there's something in a family that's been kept secret, for example, if some woman got pregnant early in life before she was married then lost the baby or gave the baby away and it never gets spoken about, that creates a trauma that will then play out in subsequent generations one way or another. Everything has a place in a family system, and everyone has to be acknowledged. Whatever the reason, be it a death, or somebody who has committed a crime that nobody wants to be associated with, families can batten down the hatches, keep that secret, which will then fester and stay in the system. They don't have to be approved of, but it must be acknowledged that they have a place in the family for that to release.

In the example I gave before of somebody looking outside the system, that could be a beloved aunt or uncle who did something terrible and then got blacklisted from the family. Yet someone in the subsequent generations is saying I'm aware of them, I can feel them. We have to include them, bring them in. When we acknowledge what is actually there in within a family system, energy moves and it can bring more peace to everyone else.

Living examples

This story happened in a constellation training that I was part of. An American woman was presenting with anorexia. She was in her 40s and had been dealing with the condition for about 20 years. The constellation was set up with quite a lot of people and what started to emerge was very much a historical aspect of her family, which slowly started to reveal that her ancestors had been slave owners in the South, which she didn't really know about.

She wasn't in the constellation herself, just observing other people representing her and different aspects of her family. And what was emerging was that they had been plantation owners with slaves, and that the women in the family had really not dealt well with the situation of the life of privilege that they had, living on the plantation, benefiting from the wealth of the plantation, while at the same time, they knew what the cost was in terms of slavery. They were put down as hysterics. They were treated as having something wrong with them, and eventually at least one, I think possibly two generations of women ended up locked up within the house on the plantation.

They were put aside because nobody wanted to deal with what they knew, what they were feeling, or anything like that.

What emerged through the story that was revealed, was that all of this energy that the women were aware of was not allowed to be expressed. There was no space for it to be received, so it was kind of backed up in them. The woman who had brought the constellation, in her way was expressing her distaste for the energy of that story by becoming anorexic, literally unable to stomach what she couldn't handle energetically. What got revealed was a shock to her. It had never been spoken about in the family. There was no record of these women having been locked up. There was no story about it at all in the family; it was unspoken and so deeply buried that she didn't even know that they were plantation owners. But it still emerged through the bodies of the subsequent generations, through the women. And that was it, that was what brought her to a constellation. What is this anorexia that she had tried lots of different things to deal with, and nothing was touching? That was the hidden story, if you like, it was the missing piece that now allowed something to settle in her. And it had a big impact on me that something like that could be buried so deep.

I had another story, also eating-related, from another workshop where there was a woman in her 30s who was Pakistani in origin and was struggling with bulimia. It was something she'd been trying to deal with. The facilitator in that one, John Payne, is particularly good with historical things so he was aware of the question - where did the family come from? They were in Pakistan, and because there had been a big migration during partition in 1948, representatives were set up for her grandmother and grandfather, and we started in India, with the grandparents before they made the journey. I was representing the grandmother in that constellation. Her parents were represented as well. They had been children at the time. And so, I was literally on this walk with them.

It was a dreadful feeling. I mean a dreadful, dreadful feeling of what we were leaving behind. We were in disbelief and didn't know what we were going through. There was complete and utter chaos all around. It was so much, and then at some point I had this feeling that I had an axe cleaving down through my crown chakra all the way down through my body. It was like I was literally being split in half. That was the feeling of walking on that road, you know, towards an unknown future where we didn't know if we'd be welcomed. We didn't know if there'd be food or anything there. And leaving behind all the heritage, all that was known and familiar. That constellation was so painful for everyone in the room, whether they were representing or not representing. It only started to resolve when John asked somebody to represent the soul of India. And when he brought the soul of India in, it felt like there was a real shift, somehow a reconnection that was possible for the people who were being forced to leave. It's almost like the soul of India didn't differentiate between the Indians and the Pakistanis, and all I remember is that it resolved the energy. It was a profound experience of what that really took for families, you know, that whole experience of partition that had seemed like a good solution to some people. The point at which constellations often resolved was when a broader context was introduced, or the soul of the people. Because the pain was so deep on a human level, it needed that bigger context to bring any kind of resolution or reframing.

I think the wrap-up was around her trying to resolve this for her grandparents. By eating she was desperately trying to fill the gap, fill the hole, fill the split in herself. Children want to take on the healing of what is sensed, but they can't do that. It is the energetic responsibility of those it happened to – the grandparents in this instance - so it has to be acknowledged and given back to them in the field."

This means that for you, in your life there can be something from the past that is affecting you now. It is in the field and it may also as a result be in the epigenes that are influencing how your DNA functions now, shaping how your body-mind functions. We will explore epigenetics more in due course. For now, please just notice how the past can remain present to us because of how it is held in the Information Field.

There's more to the past than constellations, of course. And there is more for us to engage with regarding the most foundational influences that begin our human journey. Some of them may surprise you.

That's where we are going next.

Early influences

"Before the event of birth, before we have even had a glimmer of sight or sound in the womb, we record the experience and history of our lives in our cells."

Thomas Verny on bodywide memory in "Pre-parenting"

What do you enter this world with?

Our examination of constellations marked the beginning of our challenge to the conventional view that we start with a clean slate (*tabula rasa*).

In this chapter we will add several more challenges to that conception. There is a long academic tradition of debating the "nature vs nurture" question. The purpose here is to explore just how many variables there are and to show how a theoretical debate doesn't help you in the way that looking at your own experience and self-knowledge can do.

Some of what follows may not require too much of a stretch to your way of thinking, while some may stretch it a good deal. You don't need to believe any of the ideas that I am presenting, still less all of them. However, even a few of them are likely to expand your view of yourself, and just one or two will suffice to make a mess on the slate. And I won't address them all to the same degree. In some cases I do little more than refer you to some fascinating presentations by others, not because they don't deserve fuller treatment, but because I want to preserve a strong sense of the overall theme without completely losing the richness of the picture.

Ancestral influence

Family constellations illustrate the power of influences in the field. Often what shows up is the stuff that people don't know – that which has been suppressed or hidden or simply lost to family memory. In parallel to all that are the explicit and known factors. A few hundred years ago it would be common for a young man to enter the trade of his father, grandfather and great-grandfather and become a thatcher or a mason. In many cultures, some of these are surnames that identify the family antecedents. Even now, it is not uncommon to come across farmers whose families have been on their land for five generations.

I referred earlier to my mother's career as a professional musician. Three of her close relatives were professors at the Royal Academy of Music and six more made their living through music. But there is something else just as significant. I mentioned my love of music. My older sister, now in her early eighties, sings publicly in jazz bands. You will have similar stories – families who share in supporting the same sports team, being hikers or knitters. You will know of others who are Republicans, Democrats or Tories, not because it is a political choice but because it is their identity.

Tendencies like alcoholism can blight families for generations. Some influences are less visible, and outsiders might not see them; the turn of phrase that passes from great-grandmother to three generations down, or the way that a particular recipe is prepared. You may have grown up in a family that thought higher education was for others or believed that "no Jones ever had money". These things shape you. Sometimes they may do so even when you rebel against them. They contributed to who you are. What are you aware of? And what might you not have noticed?

Genetics

There's more to say about genetics later. For now, I invite you to check your assumptions. Some things seem fixed – hair and eye colour. Some other things seem fixed, like height, but a few generations back people with very similar genes to us were shorter on average. Nutrition has made a difference. Body shape seems to run in families. But everything is complicated by having two parents. Racial typologies persist, but in varying degrees. Even something as seemingly simple as skin colour can vary significantly between siblings of mixed parentage.

There is so much we cannot see. Where does your temperament come from? Will you inherit your grandmother's susceptibility to migraines or arthritis? Or her stoic nature? The point here is to recognise how much we don't know and how much we might think we know that isn't true. When there are so many other factors at play, this may make a difference to what you can change and what choices are available to you.

Life before birth

What were you experiencing when you were in the womb? There is evidence that this matters. Here is a quote from two very experienced psychotherapists, Dr Terry Levy and Michael Orlans.

"Over the past 20 years, the new field of "foetal programming" or "foetal origins" has been studying how in utero experiences exert lasting effects on us from infancy into adulthood. A woman's experiences and lifestyle can change the development of her unborn baby and beyond. The nutrition in the womb, the drugs, infections, and pollutants the foetus is exposed to, the mother's health, stress level, and state of mind during pregnancy, all affect the foetus and the person later in life. The experience in the womb has been linked to physical and mental health problems later in life, including heart disease, diabetes, cancer, hypertension, allergies, obesity, anxiety, depression, schizophrenia, and autism."

One might expect physiological effects, but I particularly draw attention to the reference to "state of mind". If you have any sense of Information Fields, or "energies" and you consider that you were bathing in your mother's just as much as in the amniotic fluid, it is not much of a stretch to believe that these could influence you. At that stage of your existence, you have no sense of yourself as a separate being. While your mind may be in a kind of deep sleep, your brainwave patterns in the third trimester are not much different than those of a newborn. You will have heard when her heart rate increased under stress, and when she was calm. More than that, the neurochemical environment in which you were swimming would contain the many messenger chemicals that we will discuss more in a later chapter, signalling your mother's emotional state.

There is now significant evidence for the effects of such stress. As far back as 2004, the New York Times reported that researchers were finding that the foetuses of mothers who are stressed or depressed respond differently... and have a significantly increased risk of developing learning and behavioural problems. In "The Myth of Normal", Dr Gabor Maté reports multiple studies that point to the effects of emotional stress on brain structures and neurological conditions such as autism. He cites also "universal consensus" reported in one review paper, that what are called the developmental origins of adult disease begin in the womb.

At a time when loose and probably false causal associations are being made between Tylenol (Paracetamol) and autism, it is essential to observe that the use of painkillers may well be a response to those underlying stressors. More than anything, as Gabor Maté observes, it is vital to see all of these factors as in no way warranting blame of the parents, but instead the urgency and importance of ensuring the best and most supportive conditions for the mothers-to-be. Our society doesn't know how to treat this period as sacred, as would often be the case in some of the tribal societies that the West regards as "primitive". We pay the price for this.

You also heard sounds from outside. There is evidence that foetuses can recognise the father's voice from around 32 weeks into gestation. I have the belief too, that my love for a piece of music that my mother played the premiere of in the months before my birth is not entirely coincidental. But who knows? What might be possible?

Birth experience

Work in this area was pioneered independently by psychiatrist Stanislav Grof and psychotherapist Arthur Janov. Janov was highly controversial but became a celebrity with his book "The Primal Scream" and as a result of an endorsement from John Lennon.

Grof was the founder of the Holotropic Breathwork technique. At around the same time Leonard Orr developed a similar method based on a pattern of yogic breathing, which became known as "Rebirthing". It is a technique that I tried many years ago, from which I gained insights into some fundamentals of my ways of thinking and being. The theory is that when we are born, our first thoughts, emerging from the birth canal and experiencing the exterior world, lay down strong patterns that influence us throughout our lives. Examples might be that a person who experiences their mother still in pain following the birth might lay down the thought-form "Me being alive hurts women". Another who emerges into a harsh, noisy, over-bright hospital ward and experiences the intense sensations involved may form the conclusion "Being in the world is painful".

Monty Python, in their film "The Meaning of Life", portrayed a senior doctor instructing the nurse to take a mother in labour into "the foetus frightening room".[5] While I am oversimplifying, these perceptions led to changes in practice and the development of the Leboyer method. For me, decades after learning about my own conclusions through rebirthing, I had a much more intense and physical experience, prompted by a different type of real-life transition – a bereavement. My birth had been rapid and caused the thought that I would be alone, separated and abandoned. I note that this thought doesn't have to be true; I was well taken care of after only a brief period of being put down during a nursing shift change. But my bereavement experience brought those thoughts, a little later, to the surface in a stomach-clenching way. Fortunately, I was in a workshop context that created a safe psychological space for the experience. After a while to decode what was happening within me, I realised how much I felt separated, frightened inside, and wanting to scream. This is so much stronger for me than any references you might ever see to "lack of scientific evidence". The body knows what it knows, and awareness of that information releases it in the field. When I allowed myself to see, feel, witness and release what had happened, my state and my interactions with others changed. The field shifted.

---

[5] Meaning of Life https://www.youtube.com/watch?v=X04GK9DZJP0

So, your birth script might be another factor that shaped you. Do you know anything about the events of your birth? If you have any interest in ever engaging with this aspect and it is not too late to do so, it is worth asking your mother what she can remember. At the same time, I don't wish to over-emphasize its importance. It may not be significant in your life. It is simply another part of the possible story of what makes you you.

Your life as an infant

It is all too easy to think of the first years of life as passive and assume that nothing is happening that would change who we are. Little babies don't talk, and we have no idea what they think – or even if they are thinking at all. Words come much later; by the time we are articulate, few of us remember what went before. What is your earliest memory? How much of your life can you remember from those early years?

But that shouldn't mislead us. I have spent a lot of time watching babies, and what I see is that given a chance, they spend a lot of time watching us[6]. Maybe this shouldn't be surprising. There is evidence for this too, albeit limited. Infants, even before they can speak, use observation and active experience to detect regularities in others' behaviour: they link what they see others do with sensory outcomes, and over time begin to anticipate what others will do next based purely on what they have observed.[7] Animals do this too. When we think about "thinking" our attention can quickly go to the cognitive and analytical activities inside our heads. Not only is that what we are educated to do, it is also a kind of side-effect of our conscious minds. When we think about thinking, we do it with thoughts.

However obvious that might sound, the problem is what it leaves out. Animals observe and non-analytically sense patterns. I once watched a cat in my garden, crouched underneath a low wall. A

---

[6] There was an excellent BBC Series called "The World of Babies" which showed film of some research that conveys this very well, if you can find it.
[7] Based on Hunnius & Bekkering, "What are you doing?" 2014

small bird was landing there, then flying down on the other side to pick up some seeds, then coming back. The cat watched it a few times, and the next time, as the bird was landing, leapt up and scooped it into her jaws with her paw.

Cats don't analyse. Animals don't analyse in the way that we do, but they do sense patterns in their world. Little babies are the same, and patterns lead to recognition, to inferences about how life works. This person smiles at me and responds to my smile. That other person doesn't respond. My mother ignores me unless I am crying. My mother gets upset when I cry. My mother shouts when I cry.

The conventional language for this is right-brain perception. The left-brain breaks things down and sees the elements of a picture. The left brain can perform analysis and verbalize the steps. And even in animals, the left brain of the bird observed the individual seeds as it had evolved to do. They were elements in its picture. Maybe if it had been giving more attention to the whole garden it wouldn't have been the cat's lunch.

Infants are not like small adults who can't talk. Their brains are not functioning in the same way. Their brain rhythms are operating at low frequencies of 2-4 Hz, the speeds you show when you are asleep, very different from the 12Hz and above that dominate when you are awake. Not only do infants actually sleep a lot; even when awake they are in a kind of waking dream.

How many patterns had you sensed and drawn inferences from before you were one year old? I would suggest that you had some sense of the entities that comprised your world and what they caused. Your father, siblings and grandparents were distinct components that came and went throughout the day. They each behaved in recognisable ways. The one that plays, the one that talks, the one that pinches and hurts, the one that puts its face too close, the one that doesn't smell nice. How much did you know about them before they were even nameable, while they were simply aspects of your surroundings? Before you even knew yourself as a separate individual?

There is a story told by Prue Leith, a well-known UK writer and TV cook/presenter. Many years ago she adopted an orphan from the Cambodian war. When first being put to bed in her new home, Li-Da refused to give up the sausage in one fist and the fish-finger in the other. Put yourself for a moment into Li-Da's mind and experience. What might it be like to experience that intensity of starvation and fear that the food you have might not be there tomorrow? How would that affect who you are and who you become?

Your infant experiences are part of what has made you. It may take a great deal to overcome the profound sense of insecurity that such an intense early experience can instill, particularly if you were not rescued. What is the later difference for a baby who, when she cries, is always picked up, and one who is left to cry? There are many parenting theories and this is not the place to go into them. Once again, the point is to recognise that these shaping influences are there.

The significance of trauma

While not central to this book, and too big a topic to address here, it is also relevant to point out that Li-Da's experience might be seen as traumatic. There will be many times in this journey when events can occur that call for trauma-informed perspectives. You may be aware of those contexts for yourself or for others. If what I say triggers discomfort at any point, I apologise. If I don't deal with such events in greater depth, that is not to imply a diminution of their significance. Far from it.

In "The Myth of Normal", Gabor Maté explores this territory brilliantly and with depth. His strapline "Illness, health and healing in a toxic culture" signposts how he presents a detailed picture of the connecting thread through experiences, somatic responses, mindsets and cultural contexts, showing their combined results in both physical and mental illness. In doing so, he connects several layers of the Field that we are exploring, providing examples of how damage in one area has outcomes in another. However important that is, for our purposes here, it serves as an illustration of our overall context, and I will say no more, except to recommend it.

Life Between Lives and Soul Contracts

I have saved until last in this chapter, the context of life before incarnation. Even though you may have been brought up in a faith system that has a concept of "soul" and life after death (heaven or hell), or even if you accept the idea of the Dalai Lama's reincarnation, this may well be an exploration at the edge. It is a conversation that I suspect many of us find difficult to engage with, even just with ourselves.

Nevertheless, it is too powerful and important to ignore. At the centre is a simple question. Is there a "you" that has an existence beyond this incarnated lifetime? In one way or another, vast numbers of humans believe that there is. For the purposes of this section I will refer to that aspect of "you" as a soul and frame what follows around that. What you make of it is up to you.

If you are interested in going deeply into this, I recommend two books. "Journey of Souls: Case Studies of Life Between Lives" was written by Dr. Michael Newton and documents his years of practice as a psychologist and master hypnotherapist using age regression techniques to help patients address the roots of their problems. He discovered that many people would recall memories that were not from their current life and would spontaneously relive experiences from before their birth. Over 35 years he built up the patterns of evidence from 7000 clients to produce a description of what our souls engage with between one life and the next. His Institute now claims to have 55,000 records of such sessions.

The Institute's website describes an early example that prompted this body of work as follows:

In the late 1960s, Michael treated a client for psychosomatic pain of the shoulder with traditional hypnotherapy. This man had sought hypnotherapy, having exhausted the medical model where they could find nothing wrong with him. In a deep trance state, Michael asked him to go to the source of his pain, assuming some form of unconscious trauma lay beneath the condition. The client landed in a scene from WW1 where he was being bayoneted in a trench during the Battle of the Somme. Michael asked all manner of questions about his unit, commanding officer and even the badges on his uniform, before desensitizing the pain and resolving the issue. The client went away bewildered, though healed. Michael, ever the researcher, wrote to the keepers of the War Records in London and confirmed the client's story. It was a moment of deep significance and set him on the path.

As the work progressed, it became apparent that patients were remembering not just incidents from previous lives, but interactions and choices with other souls in between lives. Some of those souls were part of an ongoing group that was connected through their soul journeys across multiple lifetimes, and they were associated with the choices and intentions that individuals had set for what they wanted in the context of their current lives.

The idea of karma that is present in some religions is expanded here to include choice. We are not so much given lessons as choosing them, and we are doing so in the context of a larger perspective that is also about others and about how we collectively explore the boundaries around love, compassion and understanding. It creates a context in which our human tragedies are steps along the path of our development. In choosing, we learn about the karmic balances and take them into our future.

There are parallels between Dr Newton's work and that of Dr Caroline Myss, who is a renowned medical intuitive and spiritual teacher. In her book "Sacred Contracts" she explores the nature of the choices that we make. As she states, "*I believe that each of us is guided by a Sacred Contract that our soul made before we were born. That Contract contains a wide range of agreements regarding all that we are intended to learn in this life. It comprises not merely what kind of work we do but also our key relationships with the people who are to help us learn the lessons we have agreed to work on.*"

These contracts are agreements around our personal choices of the archetypes that we will use as the basis for our experiences. Her extensive materials provide ways to explore which archetypes you have selected and become more aware of the path that you are following.

The Information Field

I want to relate both of these descriptions to the concept of the Information Field and to our place in that field where we experience and explore our relationships with other elements of it. If you accept the premise of a soul journey, then you embrace that who you are now is in part embedded in the framework of who you have been before and who you have chosen to be now.

Where is that information held? Is it your personal property, something that your soul has custody of? Apparently not, since the agreements are made with others and are present in the universe in a way that is ongoing. It didn't merely shape where, how and to whom you were born; it is woven into the unfolding of your life and potentially influences who you will meet tomorrow. Note that this is not predetermination. It only shapes a framework of possibilities, and you continue to choose what you engage with and how you respond to whomever you meet. You may even choose whether you accept the "appointment". Otherwise, there would be no learning. This concept and this framing in the Information Field is a key component in the overall narrative, and especially in this book's eventual conclusions regarding how to get the best out of your future.

This last section has been quite short, but its implications are proportionally much bigger. It has contained an invitation to engage more closely with concepts such as karma and life after death. It asks you to consider where you stand on the question of soul, whether you have one, and what part it plays in your existence. That in its turn could lead to some re-evaluation of your relationship to death. You might retain your reluctance to die and the fears that may be there about pain and sickness. I am reminded of Woody

Allen's comment, "I don't mind dying, I just don't want to be there when it happens." Beyond that joke is something quite fundamental with big potential implications for how we approach our lives. Who has this context made you, and who might you be in the future?

What's next?

In this chapter we have focused on the individual and early influences that shape who you are. We will soon return to the thread of those influences, zooming out to a far broader perspective. But before that, I want us to take a brief look at what is in the middle, which is your physical body, your form and structure. What aspects of your being show up there, and what connections can we find between your biology and the events or conditions of your existence?

Form and Structure

Unless we can measure something, science won't concede it exists, which is why science refuses to deal with such "nonthings" as the emotions, the mind, the soul, or the spirit.

Candace Pert, Ph. D., Molecules of Emotion

You have a body. You <u>are</u> a body. In what ways are your physiological structure and your form located in the Information Field?

Throughout this book, you are at the centre of this enquiry. There is that which is outside of you in the broader field – the shape of the material universe itself. There are the aspects we have covered already, which are in the wider field in general, such as family and ancestry, together with pre-existing personal influences like soul contracts. We have begun to explore personal experience before and around birth, and there are other influences that we haven't yet come to which arise in our unique experiences when growing up as humans. Even "identical twins" differ there.

This chapter enquires into how all that shows up in our bodies. There are many connections through various aspects of our physiology. I decided to get genuine expertise into how those show up by talking to my long-term Chiropractor, Dr. Steve Williams. As you will see from the stories that follow, any image that you might have of someone who pushes bones into place is a long way from his way of working. The stories are about a holistic approach to the human body and emotions. And while I had never before had a conversation with Steve explicitly about the Information Field, you will see how what he says endorses and illustrates that perspective.

Steve is deeply experienced and as the stories will illustrate, has studied and uses a range of health modalities and is hugely informed. He also has a speciality in paediatrics and is the author of an authoritative textbook and a lecturer worldwide on the subject. Accordingly, his first story is about a baby.

I am thinking of a child, one of the worst infants I've seen, a vomiting, refluxy infant, a screaming child who was not passing stool. Anybody who has experience of babies, knows those who don't poo regularly are generally not happy. They need to be clearing their system a few times a day. This one was not pooing, was straining all the time, was poseting (small vomits) after feeding and just seemed angry.

It is really interesting because it wasn't the mother's first child so she knew that this baby was different, and anyway how can a baby be angry? It might be something that we say, but babies are not inherently angry. This was just a very upset child who was in an ongoing stress response, screaming, crying, could not be left alone, or put down.

And even when held it would be angsty, and not comfortable, and the key factor for mum was that she was unable to comfort her child. She said "there's something going on with this child; my previous one wasn't like this". So then we looked at what happened during the pregnancy and birth. The mum had an enormous emotional issue creating a major stress response during her pregnancy. That huge emotional issue was death of a parent and she went through a terrible time. As a result, what was going on in her system? It was just a highly, highly stressful time.

So part of actually dealing with that infant was gentle cranial and spinal adjusting to activate the vagus nerves which are the main part of the parasympathetic nervous system, the rest and recuperation nervous system. That poor baby was fixed in fight or flight. When stuck in fight or flight, it can either make the bowels very loose or just stop working. That child was pooing very infrequently and subsequently straining, increasing abdominal pressure and was then bringing some of it back.

So, what was needed, alongside me doing some work on that fight or flight stuff, was also the mum coming together and rebonding with the child. It turned out that delivery hadn't gone well and ended up in a Caesarean-section. We know that caesarean births miss out on the squeezing and compression in the birth canal which is part of awakening their physicality as they transition from floating in the cushion of fluid in the amniotic sac. So one of the things we do with children who've been in a C-section is get the parents to do a strip, head-to-toe, gentle, compressive massage. Some oil (extra virgin coconut is great) is used for lubrication in a nice, quiet environment, one parent holding the little one, the other strip massaging from the crown of the head, where their head would come through the birth canal, right the way down to the toes, in short 4-5cm strips down through the body, arms, legs to each finger and toe. The whole procedure should take only 12 to 15 minutes.

It is then a lovely idea to have baby lying on the mum, skin to skin, on her chest. The baby can feed if it wants, doesn't matter, they just have some together bonding time. Maternal guilt for the baby having issues can be huge, and this is when I suggest the mum tries to lose some of it at least. It has been no one's fault and just one of those hurdles life can throw in our path Heaven knows, when you have massive stresses in your life, you're going to be stressed. It's just one of those things.

And then, as she described to me, because it was just her and her partner there, it felt like almost a rebirthing moment. There were lots of emotions - the mum was crying, the baby was also crying very, very gently. The infant became much easier to work on and within a week or so was pooing, was happier, was less sick, and less in that fight or flight, and became a baby that was no longer what the mother described as really angry.

In that, one of the learnings I've had showed up, pointing up that linkage between the mum and the baby. You can cut that umbilical cord; there is still that emotional, energetic attachment of that cord. It's one of those reasons why I really do encourage mums to take as much time off work as they can, certainly in the first six months, ideally a year, but if they can do six months, that initial time when the baby is essentially still so dependent. The nearer to mum the infant can be the better, the mum's voice, breathing rhythms, heart sounds and probably electromagnetic fields are all sources of reassurance and comfort for the young infant. And of course, it's part of the time that mums - you want to try and de-stress your life as much as you can and just enjoy that moment, because it's your chance of bringing a new human being truly into the world. They're born, but then they really become that individual over the first six to 12 months. That story of the little one discussed above taught me a massive amount about what happens with those emotional maternal-baby interactions. This is not meant to make any mum feel guilty, for pity's sake. We all go through these things and they've all got to be regarded as just lessons for our lives.

That is a really good example in this book's context because of the number of different strands that illustrate what I have been talking about – the connection between mother and child, the in utero experience, the fact that healing takes place in the space between them, in the relational space. It depicts the way all aspects of the exterior events and inner relationships flow through their combined systems, and how all the information about that is contained within them and in the Information Field. That's also where the ancestral stuff, where every bit of our histories is sitting, and this story nicely illustrated where those different parts of the field are being impacted.

So I asked Steve to take the story forward into what he has seen in adults, and to get a sense of the internal connections between different aspects of the body-mind. This is where he took that question.

Yes, adults are very interesting from that perspective. Babies are, if you like, simpler, more direct, and with fewer layers baked in over the years. Adults are inherently more complex. Here is one we can use as an illustration because we've got a few of them and they're all pretty complex. But I'll pick this individual who was a big, tough rugby player years before, really physical with all that you might associate with that image. Then he developed low back pain and neck pain. He'd had significant physical trauma at various times over the years, but he wouldn't come in until he was eventually persuaded to by his wife.

In the end I found out why he didn't want to come in was because he didn't like being touched. He didn't like anybody touching him and his wife mentioned this. I found that if I tried to touch him, he was covered in sweat, really stressed and would not release anything, just couldn't release tension in his system. If I'd put him onto his side to try and adjust him, he would be rigid, so there was very little point in doing much physical stuff to him because it wasn't going to do much.

He had had, by this stage, back surgery for disc prolapse. Now he was in the situation of having a post-surgical low back problem because a lot of the time, five to ten years post-disc surgery, the discs above and below can start giving some issues because the original problem was never taken care of.

This guy had the most defensive movement pattern. He was a tough bloke, a big physical character who loved smashing into people on the rugby pitch. But we had to start doing some other techniques because there's very little point in jumping on someone's back if they're not going to let anything happen to them. So I said to him, "Look, I'm going to do some other techniques with you." And we started going through some kinesiology and a method called BEST (Bio-Energetic Synchronisation Technique), where we can potentially ask the body what's going on without engaging with the symptoms.

It emerged that this all went back to a trauma when young, when he had been abused, and that had really created such a huge anxiety. So you can understand why he wouldn't want anybody touching him and why he was anxious about it. At the same time, he was a hell of a big, strong man and wanted to prove himself, so he went into the toughest, hardest sport he could in order to do that. So, we had to then use some techniques designed to work on memory patterns to try and deal with that. I also suggested he did some EMDR (Eye-Movement Desensitisation and Reprocessing), which finds and shifts the relevant memory patterns in the brain. With the combination of us and the EMDR, he became a lot more relaxed about being touched and about movement. He started releasing his system a lot more, and in the end, he gradually got better and out of those pain syndromes.

It wasn't using those physical high-velocity adjustments people associate with chiropractors. There's no point in doing that if someone is going to resist everything because of their old patterns, and it would have been a temporary relief, because this guy was in defence from issues that happened to him when he was very, very young. And, it was stuff that I don't think even his wife knew about at the time because he hadn't said anything, but he actually ended up talking about it and became, from her perspective, a much easier individual to live with. He became less uptight about many things in life.

That example is about a direct emotional trauma someone has had in their life but the more difficult ones are ones where it goes down generations, and you don't know why you feel like you do. You don't know why you're as resistant and as anxious and as uptight in many aspects of life. Why do you have anxiety unrelated to what would be a normal stress response for your life? Yet these are things that we see all the time, and with kinesiology and other such techniques, we can often change those patterns in the brain, which can really be helpful. This means that some of the time we work with therapists, psychologists or psychiatrists because they need other input as well.

Yes. Thank you.

Steve, I think it would be helpful maybe just to hear in your words and in the context that you're describing, how you would say that kinesiology is operating?

Okay, so kinesiology is basically about the relationship between muscle strength and weakness and how we can use this to identify areas where there are issues in the body that need addressing. Applied kinesiology was developed by Dr. George

Goodhart, and since then other strands have come from it, such as Applied Kinesiology, Touch For Health, and a myriad of other techniques.

He found that there are various points in the body which relate to organ systems, drainage systems and other bodily functions. So you can use the strength or weakness of a muscle – say the arm when asking a question about the liver, or spleen or whatever by touching the relevant point on the body and holding an inquiry about its state. Is it functioning well or not? The points may be associated with the traditional Chinese acupuncture points, which themselves come from original points that were recognised by the Indus Valley civilization thousands of years ago. This system can be very useful giving indicators of when and where to treat the patient involving organ systems, structure, energetics and the cranium.

You might ask, now, how does that work? What happens so that one part of the body can tell you about another that is not obviously related? There are various theories. One, that it is proprioceptive, that there is an abnormal proprioception-abnormal firing of muscles, abnormal firing of joint fibres in the area, so touch them, you stretch the muscles over the area, and that causes a strong muscle to become weak.

I subscribe more to the energetic theory personally, which is that we have an energetic body around us and within that energetic body we will have areas of altered energetic function related to whether the organs are working appropriately, for example whether your brain's working appropriately, whether that shoulder's working appropriately alters the electromagnetic field.[8]

---

[8] There is scientific evidence for both the theories that Stephen describes. Koncz et al. in "Postural Responses in Trauma-Experience Individuals" described that people with histories of trauma show altered **proprioception** (awareness of body position), difficulties in balance, higher muscle tone, and dissociative symptoms. Bessel van der Kolk, in "The Body Keeps the Score" said "Traumatized people chronically feel unsafe inside their bodies: The past is alive in the form of gnawing interior discomfort."

So now you're talking about the Field with the knowledge of the universe being in the Field and everything in it being in the Field. You have your own field, which interacts with everybody else's field, which interacts with the universal field. And the more we work with that, the more we can understand it. Kinesiology is a way of tapping in, in my opinion, to what's happening within your individual field. That means we can ask questions of it. So you can even ask yes or no questions that aren't about the body because your muscles can feed back awareness of what is in the field beyond.

I know this is quite difficult for a lot of people to grasp if you don't have an understanding or an interaction with that field system, but it's what we can do. I did think it was pretty strange when I first came across it. But then when you when you get to use it, it becomes so valuable to be able to ask questions of the body and get answers, and it's been one of the most useful techniques. I've been using it now for 40 years. A lot of the time it will surprise you because you can ask, is this area where they're getting pain the problem or is it somewhere else? And often what you are seeing will be secondary to other areas in the system, so we can find and treat those areas because they are the cause of the dysfunction. One of the dangers for anybody who's working in any therapy, any healing modality, is getting led by symptoms. Instead of following the symptoms, you can go into the issues beneath. Of course, we want to know what's going on with the patient, we want them to tell us where their pain is. We want them to tell us what is showing up, but then we need to have ways of following the chain and trying to find out where the major dysfunctions are, and that's what kinesiology, I think, can do for us.

Thanks. I love the yes and no questions. I use kinesiology all the time, like when deciding what to eat in restaurants. What does my body want? What will be good here?

Yes, 100%. You can use the O-ring test where you hold your thumb and first finger closed and see if that stays firm in relation to the question. It's probably the most validated test in kinesiology. It's been shown in so many research studies in Japan.

I didn't know that, but certainly it's worked for me in all sorts of ways. It's so elegant and so quick as a decision-making tool.

Totally. Totally. And you get better at it when you practice, because, you know, part of the thing is, you've got to accept it may give you the answer you don't want. Otherwise we could over-influence the response, but you can get past that. I do it fast, you know, like, yes, no, okay, and then it's a question of, is this food going to be good for me today? Yes. Should I eat that one? No. Okay. Done. Okay. I don't want to know more.

And knowing how to get your head out of the way. I think that's where the practice comes in, finding that space where your conscious thinking isn't involved and then being able to trust because you know you've got your head out of the way. It's one of the great forms of magic from my point of view, to be able to tap into what my body knows in that way.

It's simple magic and it's stuff anybody can learn. It works. But what I did with lots of that is actually go through it and say, okay, how am I going to follow up? How am I going to use this? What's going to work? In practice the O-ring test is as accurate as anything else and allows us to tap into that little bit of knowledge of the field, that little bit of knowledge within us. And it gets to a point when you are good enough at it and in a clear space, you know what your muscle is going to say. Before I do the test, I know what it's going to be. That's tuning into the Field in a different way. And I'm quite convinced we can all tune in in that way. We can get that universal knowledge. Dr John Upledger, who developed craniosacral therapy (CST) talked about it, about talking to your inner physician. And what is your inner physician? - it's the Field. That's your inner physician, it's inner and outer, and it's everywhere.

That is the ultimate beauty of it.

Thank you, Steve.

It feels appropriate with that mention of Upledger to close this chapter with a personal story that connects to CST. A few decades ago, I was receiving CST treatment. It was perhaps my second or third session. CST works with the rhythms of the cerebrospinal fluid. The practitioner feels and adjusts the movements of these with his hand around the back of the client's head and his fingers in the   occipital   region.

A little way into the session, my practitioner said to me, "Are you circumcised?", which seemed at the time like an odd question, and I wondered where he was coming from with it, but I answered, "Yes". I was born at a time when some doctors, and my parents, who seem not to have known any better, were under the delusion that evolution had made a mistake, and that its design for the human penis was faulty and unhygienic. In a way, I regard myself as having been the infant subject of male genital mutilation.

I am not telling this story as a whinge. Even if I disapprove of the practice, I am OK now with the way I am. What struck me at the time, and still amazes me, is that he could tell something that had happened decades earlier to a distant appendage from something as seemingly unconnected as spinal fluid. The significance of that pattern was understood through the CST method as "circumcision trauma", and it was known to result in a subtle shift in the way someone affected would hold their body. For me it was an early and very tangible example of the way in which bodily systems are connected. It relates to this book's presentation and this chapter's theme of how our physiological structure holds information about who we are. That kind of connection fills our bodily memory and the energetic shaping of who we are. Once again, we encounter an element of what makes you, YOU.

What's next?

What if there is another aspect to the Information Field? What if you are shaped by the timing and cosmological context of your birth? What if that shaping could extend all the way to the genetics that you begin with and the way that those will be influenced day by day and year by year?

We are moving towards an exploration which covers connections all the way from the solar system to your DNA. On the way, we need to take a brief look at DNA itself and create a framework for its relationship with various environments, as the centre of how we physiologically present ourselves, and how that impacts our behaviour.

Genetics: Form, Structure and Being

"The moment you change your perception is the moment you rewrite the chemistry of your body."

Dr. Bruce Lipton, author of "The Biology of Belief"

This chapter could be a very long one, or relatively short, and it will have to be the latter[9]. Even so, this piece of the story holds a central position in the overall picture since you are, after all, an incarnated being.

I want to go straight to the core of the issue, which is that for most of the seven decades since Franklin, Watson and Crick discovered the double helix mechanism, genes have been presented to us as the blueprint for who we are. We have been misled. The blueprint of your house did not tell you how it looked or how the builders built it. The engineer's drawing of your car contains no fuel and does not tell you what it is like to drive it.

The key elements in this mythology are:-

- There is a chemical code that controls the process by which cells replicate and organisms develop

- Sequences of those chemicals can be identified and are called "genes"

- Those sequences are associated with particular outcomes in the body, or characteristics, leading to the idea that you can have "a gene for cancer" or that there is a gene responsible for being left-handed or for Mozart's genius

- Everything about our development is dictated by our genes, by the sequence of chemicals contained in our

---

[9] Chapters 9 and 10 of Science of Possibility provide the detailed background

chromosomes.

The first two are partly true. The others are not. Most characteristics are the result of complex interactions between multiple genes. Nor are characteristics always in your own genes. An example of this occurs in snails, whose shells are formed in spirals. They coil either clockwise or counterclockwise. There is indeed a detectable genetic factor, but it is not in the organism. The gene is in the parent. That is, there appears to be a gene which says "this organism's offspring will (or will not) coil clockwise". The effect of the gene is delayed by one generation.

Ask yourself too, what did it take for you to grow as you did? What did it take to construct mechanisms such that a six-year-old loses and replaces her front teeth, but not her molars? What is needed to instruct a 14-year-old boy to grow facial hair but not grow breasts, expand his voice-box, widen his shoulders but not his pelvic girdle? What causes process to stop as well as start - what determines when these events are deemed to be complete? Why am I not 8 feet tall, and why aren't you still growing?

And then, if you treat genes as a code, where and what is the code-reader? In the snail-coiling example, it turns out that development involves an interaction between the instructions supplied in the cell nucleus and other factors supplied by the mother in the egg's environment. The reality is that living processes depend on many, many features that make it possible for us to cope with variations in our environment – some which help keep organisms in a certain range (like maintaining a stable temperature) and others that cause us to vary. In enclosed environments like the Eden Project or the Biosphere, growers were obliged to shake the trunks of saplings regularly to ensure that the trees were stimulated to produce adequate root systems. When you think about it, this is quite a subtle mechanism involving not a one-off "switch" but a progressive series of responses over time.

If you need any more convincing about whether your genes make you who you are, consider this fact. Fruit flies have 15,000 genes, nematode worms have 24,000 and rats about 25,000. You too have about 25,000 genes.

After half a century of assumed genetic determinism, science has moved towards an understanding that DNA does not have primacy. There is a sophisticated interplay of blueprint and environment, just as our earlier examples indicated should be expected. It is like the distinction between the hardware of your TV set and the programs that are transmitted through it. You can change what the TV set shows by switching channels. Equally, you can change the appearance of the program displayed on the screen by altering colour and contrast settings. The two are interdependent. There are several identified mechanisms that have the equivalent effect in modifying what you see as the outcome of cellular development. The picture is so much more complex than most stories we are presented with. We would like it to be simple, but it isn't. There is a reason why billions spent on finding a cure for cancer have produced progress, but no magic bullet.

You have something like 40 trillion cells. That is a number which I have been writing for decades and still can't get my head around. I would be impressed if you can. This matters because each cell has a life of its own. Each one has its internal living chemistry, and each is contained in a membrane that controls how those processes are both affected by and protected from what is happening in the cell's environment. The cell itself is the result of events starting around 2 billion years ago where different single-celled organisms combined to create more complex and internally co-operative processes. Those more complex forms enabled more design possibilities, including the ability to combine into multi-cellular structures like us. New layers of relationship were added bit by bit, over time.

Combining units to create larger structures is a principle of living systems. Proteins formed amino-acids, which created cells, organs, structures (like a skeleton and connective tissue) and birds, reptiles and mammals. As a highly influential mammal, some of our impact has arisen from our way of combining into social structures. This has enabled an additional level of adaptability. In turn, our psychology has been part of that adaptation as we will see later. This aspect of life does not stop, and we continue to create new relationships with the whole, all of which feeds into this book's conclusions about what is next for us.

You are already a collective. Within our bodies, cells are maintaining themselves and they are also maintaining us. But in addition to that environmental regulation, they are also working together to create our "behaviour". Collectively they allow us to walk, talk, eat, and have sex. There is collective "doing stuff". The power of these big cellular collectives greatly exceeds that which the cells possess individually.

We are not used to thinking about the way in which trillions of cells achieve this collectivisation. We are accustomed to imagining that decisions are made in our brains and that muscles act to carry them out. We are led to believe that our brains work out what to do and then we do it. Not so.

We have been offered a model of the brain as a kind of computer, connected to a nervous system, so that the brain can make decisions and control everything. That image is embedded in our culture and language and mindsets. There is another reality, however. Your body is filled with messenger chemicals. We know that that cells in every part of the body have receptors, usually for many different messengers, sometimes acting in combination. But those chemical messengers do not all come from the brain. All these cells, all over the body, are not only receiving messages; they are also sending them. Peptides, messenger molecules, are being produced everywhere. The brain is not the centre of this process; it is but one among many organs, all of which play a part in regulating physical processes. Our bodies are like a society of cells.

Once you grasp the scale and intricacy of these interactions, it becomes apparent that the body is <u>mind all over</u>. There is so much more happening besides our mental process. You may think that it is your brain which tells your lungs that it is time to breathe, but multiple control systems are working together. And then you have to know that it's not just physical. The researcher who broke the ground on this awareness of messenger hormones, Candace Pert, called her book "Molecules of Emotion" and her book is filled with the many ways in which this shows up[10].

---

[10] Molecules of Emotion. "To cite just one recent example, Rita Valentino of the University of Pennsylvania has shown that the nucleus of Barrington in the hindbrain, formerly believed to control merely micturition (bladder-emptying), sends axons containing the neuropeptide CRF down through the vagus nerve all the way to the most distant part of the large intestine, near the anus. Rita has proved that sensations of colonic distension (i.e. the feeling of needing to poop) as well as those of genital arousal are carried back to the nucleus of Barrington. From there, there is a short neuronal pathway (called a "projection") that hooks up to the locus coreolus, the nor-epinephrine-containing source of the "pleasure pathway", which is also very high in opiate receptors. The pleasure pathway hooks up to the control area of these bathroom functions, which is located in the front of the brain. Goodness, is it any wonder, based on Rita's neuro-anatomical discoveries, that toilet training is loaded with emotional stuff! Or that people get in to some unusual sexual practices involving bathroom behaviours! Clearly the classical psychologists had grossly underestimated the complexity and scope of the neurochemistry and neuroanatomy of the autonomic nervous system. But the limitations of the past are now giving way before our newfound ability to track these fascinating connections.

If we accept the idea that peptides and other informational substances are the biochemicals of emotion, their distribution in the body's nerves has all kinds of significance, which Sigmund Freud, were he alive today, would gleefully point out as the molecular confirmation of his theories. The body is the unconscious mind! Repressed traumas caused by overwhelming emotion can be stored in a body part, thereafter affecting our ability to feel that part or even move it. The new work suggests there are almost infinite pathways for the conscious mind to access – and modify – the unconscious mind and the body, and also provides an explanation for a number of phenomena that the emotional theorists have been considering."

Since the messenger chemicals are produced everywhere in the body, they are also found on the cells of the immune system. The cells which are carried in the bloodstream and that detect and destroy disease-producing organisms are as much a part of the communications process as any other. This in turn has led to one aspect of Dr. Bruce Lipton's work, which is the recognition that your thoughts and emotions show up in the deeper functioning of your body and in the maintenance of your health. It's in the title of his book "The Biology of Belief", which has become a seminal text in our understanding of how this works, and it is encapsulated in the quote at the head of this chapter.

He is explaining the mechanisms for something that humans have known for a long time. The perception that the whole body is active, that it behaves like a hologram in which any part holds information about the whole, that the body is a holistic system in which all organic processes are interrelated, is fundamental to all complementary health and natural-tradition medical systems. The relevance of Relational Being to this book's context is that all those holistic systems share a core perception that the process is also connected with the spirit - in all senses of that word. They would include the spiritual well-being of the individual - their overall emotional tone. They would include the notion that a spiritual entity exists – spirit in the sense of what might be called a soul. They would include spirit in the sense of a relationship with a wider energy world, a relationship which might be felt with nature, with ancestors, with the land, or with the "Divine", whether that be expressed as a supreme being or one of the other formulations that describe that realm.

This frame of connectivity feeds into our next chapter, because from the centre of our physicality we are about to zoom out, firstly into who we are as a social collective, then into nature and eventually into how we connect to the widest context of all. What is our relationship with the cosmos, and how does that shape who we are individually? Can we connect the cosmos to our DNA, and what might that look like?

Sooner or later, it's going to get epic.

Expanding into US

"I believe the astonishingly consistent and nuanced reality of the planetary correlations with the archetypal dynamics of human life is one of the most compelling intimations we have that we live in a meaning-laden and purposeful universe."

— *Richard Tarnas, Cosmos and Psyche*

Moving beyond the individual

Our explorations so far have concentrated on personal influences. They have been about your experiences and your choices. Even if, as with the "soul" question, they have not been inside the boundaries of what you might normally consider to be "you", they have been about you as an individual.

This also applies to the context for astrology and Gene Keys, all of which we have yet to explore. However cosmic the background and however much embedded in the Information Field that spans all of existence, you are unique. Your configuration is yours alone. Even if someone else shares your exact time of birth, they cannot share your place.

Each new piece of our jigsaw carries significant implications for who you are and, since you are an action, who you be and who you are being. There is a good chance that this story has already gone well beyond your previous notions of identity and your concepts of what has shaped you. I hope we are also expanding your sense of who you can yet become. Aware or not, we are all becoming. We will not be the same tomorrow. As Heraclitus said, you cannot step into the same river twice because the river is not the same river, and you are not the same you. But what, in this context, is the river?

The River of We

No man is an island,
Entire of itself;
Every man is a piece of the continent,

A part of the main.

If a clod be washed away by the sea,
Europe is the less,
As well as if a promontory were:
As well as if a manor of thy friend's
Or of thine own were.

Any man's death diminishes me,
Because I am involved in mankind.
And therefore never send to know for whom the bell tolls;
It tolls for thee.

This poem by John Donne contains a breadth of vision that extends into the ideas of oneness and of the entire field. It presents us as connected in ways that would have been beyond the science or cosmology of his time. In that sense it is a frame for this whole book, but I bring it in now with a simpler context. We grow up in the context of other people, and there are collective influences on us that are shared.

Degrees of Separation

As we enter this territory, it is helpful to notice that if you are swimming or even floating in a river, some parts of it are close to you and some parts are farther away. While the whole river may shape the overall direction of travel, there are eddies and currents closer to you that influence where you go – whether you get pushed towards the bank, or onto rocks. Not everything that will be described here is equal. Similarly, your own movements, what you do with your hands or legs, also affect the movement of waters that are close to you without changing the river as a whole. You might affect fish or crustaceans that you don't even see.

The river is a metaphor for how you are as an entity in the Information Field. In the field, you don't have hands and feet, and the boundary is less defined. Instead, you have the information that flows within you and through you. You are part of the river. Your own thoughts are information events that can alter the content of the field. They are the equivalents of hands and feet. Your choices make a difference.

Relational Being

As I will regularly repeat, our existence is an exercise in Relational Being. Being part of the river, we are never far from the paradox of being simultaneously in the Oneness of everything that is while seeing and experiencing ourselves as distinct. You have a sense of a boundary such that not only are you distinct from me, a different individual, but that you are also separate from everything that is beyond the boundaries of your own skin.

At the same time, there is oxygen in the air outside of your body, some of which will be breathed in and will become part of your bloodstream, transported by the haemoglobin of your red cells to chemically combine with other atoms and be part of your body. Later, some of those atoms will be expelled from your body as CO_2, to be used by your houseplants, converted into sugars which when they are used as fuel, will in turn liberate that oxygen to the air. You are a flow.

This is another metaphor for the Information Field, and for the truth that life takes place, not in you, but in the interactions between you and everything other than you. At a less granular level life is happening in the relationships that I have with objects in my environment, the people I am connected to, and the events in the world. I am in continuous interaction with the keyboard I am typing on. Life is not happening to me or from me, but in the spaces between me and all the parts that are not me. The parts that are living make such interactions more visibly two-way. This becomes the essence of what follows here, the aspects of US and of the

WHOLE which affect my own flows. Our story has not left the core question of what makes you YOU.

The first layer of "Us"

Most of us grow up in families, with a parent or two and maybe siblings. If not, you have an equivalent – the people with whom you spent your formative years, the ones whom you observed during your infancy, maybe from a pre-verbal space, but subsequently those from whom you learned not only language but basic customs, rhythms and habits such as when you ate and what kinds of food, or what people talked about. Often just as importantly, what they never, ever talked about.

It is sometimes said that fish have no concept of water. Maybe that is so, at least until they are out of it and notice its absence. Either way, I offer this as an image of our early life in the sense that we are typically unaware of what we are absorbing into ourselves. Not only may it be pre-verbal and non-verbal, but because it is built into the fabric of our existence there is nothing to think about. It simply IS, and that means we easily overlook it. Nevertheless, you may wish to give some thought to how much there is to add alongside our earlier thoughts about what comes from our ancestors. Of course, some aspects of our family environment may include what has been passed down to them, but you might like to give some consideration to what you have taken on as part of you without much choice, and when you had no filters to apply to the process.

Sometimes it can be helpful to reflect on this question by considering all the things you are not, and perhaps how difficult it is to imagine growing up in an entirely different context. We tend to assume that other people must think the same way that we do, even our neighbours, despite how different our conclusions and behaviours turn out to be. But although I have visited countries which are very hot, I can't really imagine what it would be like to have grown up in an African village where people cook outdoors on open fires. What is the internal world of an Inuit like, raised in igloos and surrounded by snow and ice? What would it be like to encounter your first tree or flower at the age of six?[11]

I don't remember anything at all from before the age of three. But the more I have considered what I know of myself at four and five, the more I can see that was already built into my being by then.

How is that for you?

The second layer of "Us"

Even as little children our immediate family is not all we encounter. We may be among extended families, taken to community events and festivals. We grow up with the rhythms of festivals, Christmas treats or Ramadan fasts. We are in neighbourhoods that may be anything from immigrant enclaves to the diversity of modern urban mixes. We may be born with mixed parentage and witness two quite different sets of grandparents and cousins.

Does it make a difference to attend a Christian church or a Synagogue at that age? Does it matter whether your mother sang snatches of opera or the American songbook while cooking, or what station the radio was tuned to? What feels significant to you?

Communal or tribal influences go deep. I could give a hundred examples and merely skim the surface. And besides the content of the local culture, the nature of connectedness varies. Some communities are close-knit, whole villages, even urban ones, where many besides kin are involved in raising a child. Others, the result of recent decades with greater geographical and social mobility, new towns and modern suburbs, may have very little sense of such cohesion. Depending on the nature of where and how you were brought up, your experience may have been different mixes of these. What did your early years make you?

And lastly please note that you may have had an experience of rejecting your parents, your family or your wider "tribe". If so, don't make the mistake of thinking that they didn't shape you. Even what

[11] https://www.youtube.com/watch?v=C3upRQID1tw

you reject is formative and even the interior dynamics of the rejection remain alive in your being. For example, none of the tacitly lapsed or even firmly rejecting ex-Catholics I have met would say that there are no lasting implications. Indeed, they complain of just the opposite.

Religious systems

Religious systems are more than personal experiences. They inhabit the ways of thinking for entire nations. Even now, when so many Western countries that 50 years ago would have been seen as Judeo-Christian may have experienced immigration from areas dominated by Hindu or Islamic faiths, and even though church attendances have dwindled, a Christian ethos still runs through the collective. We have a shared history for the meaning of "God", a concept of justice, a residual Protestant work ethic. We all shut down for Christmas; our shops pipe the music of "Little Donkey" and "Mary's Boy Child". Santa Claus was based on a Christian saint. You might say that even those who no longer attend church know what religion they are not practising, and atheists know what kind of God they are choosing not to believe in.

What do you see in your background? If you are not aligned with a particular faith, can you nevertheless detect the influence of one on what surrounds you in family, community or nation, and how that contributes to the way you see the world? Despite being raised by atheists I am in no doubt about the influences on my morality. It takes intention and effort for me not to connect the word "God" to an old man with a white beard and a pointy finger. I am tainted by Michelangelo. We all grow up with iconography of some kind. And since the musical family background I mentioned earlier was rooted in the classical genre, I learned early to resonate with composers like Bach and Mozart. No matter how much my tastes later extended into jazz or rock, or even ragas, their faith hums in my bones.

Primary Education

Schooling is another way that we are all shaped. Maybe this is so obvious as to require no elaboration. But I invite you to ponder it personally for a moment. Remember that our core enquiry is into what makes you you. You were probably not taught to think in hexadecimal numbering because the decimal system is so universal. It is as hard to imagine us having sixteen fingers. But maybe you can conceive of a sci-fi scenario in which we encounter an alien civilization who are different at such a fundamental level, maybe having three limbs each with four manipulating ends, for whom triangles are more natural than squares and whose architecture is all constructed without right angles. That's not so far-fetched; an octopus has part of its brain distributed through its eight limbs. If it invented arithmetic, that might be octal.

While your parents may well have taught you how to behave, your school will most likely have taken whatever variability that involved and homogenised it into something that is held in common. We are socialised as well as educated – some would say more than. Maybe your view of what discipline and self-discipline look like will have been shaped as your milk teeth were replaced by your adult ones.

While that was happening in the background, the foreground began to shape your view of nature, of the planets and of what scientific knowledge believes the world to be. This book presents a different view of reality. In presenting the concept of an information-driven universe and asking you to engage with it as a new way of seeing, I am challenging years of indoctrination.

Wider Culture

Humans share so much. Soccer is worldwide. Have you ever seen the credits at the end of a Netflix series listing all the actors who dubbed the voices into different languages? Thanks to Squid Game and K-Pop we in the West can all have new connections to South Korea. Or maybe you are a Korean reading this paragraph.

We are in a transition where, depending on your age, where you have come from, how much you have travelled and your level of curiosity, you can have been exposed to a myriad of influences. The growth in possibilities has been exponential. There are African children who know the names of Manchester City footballers, some of whom may indeed be African. Every year we are nations less and Earthers more. The Star Trek scenarios of spaceships crewed not only by multiple nationalities, but by Vulcans and Klingons, are not that big a stretch to our concepts of who we are.

Amid this transition, you are who you are. The process that made you that, is not finished. We are all being reshaped and we can all reshape ourselves. I see it as essential to recognise that this transition to a global awareness is now critical to our future. Climate change and Covid19 alike have pushed us towards the need to act together against the folly of behaving as if we don't all share the same air supply. Expanding into Us was both a title/perspective for this chapter and a description of our shared human challenge. I will return to this topic later when talking about our future choices. All the shapers are helpful to know about because the more we can see, the more freedom we gain to step away from them.

We still have many more shapers to engage with. In the next chapter we will visit some more of the individual ones, but as this book progresses, we will engage increasingly with the way we have built our world around us and with what we can change. We are not stuck with who we are nor with what we have.

What else is possible?

What's Nature to You?

"A mycelial network is a map of a fungus's recent history and is a helpful reminder that all life-forms are in fact processes not things. The "you" of five years ago was made from different stuff than the "you" of today. Nature is an event that never stops."

Merlin Sheldrake, Author of "Entangled Life"

You could have a wide range of conscious responses to the title question, from "everything" to "almost nothing." The modern world brings disconnection to so many of us, living in urban environments, travelling by car, living in apartments without even a garden. We might create some measure of connection by owning a pet dog or being in service to a resident cat. Maybe we can find a green space or open water at the weekend. Maybe we tend a garden, or planters on our balcony.

How does the header question land with you? Even its form places us as separate from nature as if we ourselves are unnatural; we are part of nature, whether or not we think so. Regardless, we might enjoy TV nature programs. There is some astonishing film of creatures we would never see, in environments that we will never visit. We can witness the richness and magnificence, the wonder of creation, but at a distance, through a screen. It's in our heads but not our bodies.

There are areas of public discourse where to be called a "tree hugger" is an insult. Humans have cut down forests in huge numbers. To many, land is merely a resource; feeling that you can connect to a tree is ridiculed as borderline insanity. Yet many people, if asked to talk about a favourite tree would come up with a lived experience, maybe a memory, but often one that is current for them. Do you have one? Perhaps, like me, you are proud to be a tree hugger. Likewise, there are places that we connect to, maybe hold in our hearts for years without necessarily visiting again. Even the memory can nourish us at a deep level. Maybe that is also true for you. Can you, like me, name certain places that you know contain some special quality, more than just surface beauty, a feeling that speaks to your soul and feeds your spirit.

How deep does this go?

I know how I feel about certain regions of England because of the shape of the land. I think it dates from when I lived in the foothills of the Mendips at the age of 7 to 11, and it developed further after that when we moved to the Cotswolds. I now feel that sensation in other, similar areas; hills touch me. In contrast, living in Arizona for two years was like a deprivation. I acknowledge that those areas of desert full of Saguaro and Prickly Pear are also magnificent in their way. Objectively, I recognise their stark beauty, and they are no less natural. I used to hike Camelback Mountain near Scottsdale, and that was grand too, but none of these features ever touched me much. When I came back to England, I felt myself sucking up the green in a huge energetic inhalation that lasted several days. It is how I imagine that a drug addict feels when they have been without a fix – maybe not so desperate, but intense in its own way - though in contrast to the addict who knows what they have been missing, I only recognised it when it was there again.

Does this resonate at all for you? I am still orienting what I say around this book's central theme. The way that I am describing my experience makes it clear that the land has shaped me. It is also apparent from the stories they tell that many people who grow up in mountains or by the sea feel similarly deprived if they can't be there. I hear farmers talking about the land their families have worked for generations as the most beautiful place on God's earth, even while they are on the news because there's a blizzard or a flood, and it looks inhospitable to me. For many people this goes very deep indeed, like a taproot.

Getting beneath the surface

Returning to the "tree huggers" this is not only about having an affection for particular trees. Like everything else in this book it's about the Field and about spirit. Referring to an Information Field can sound a bit dry, which it isn't at all. Just as the Information Field in you adds up to a person, a being and a spirit, so it is for the tree. If you are a tree hugger, you may know the experience of each tree as a distinct individual. Our intuitive sensing, our gut-feel, our knowing comes into play. If you don't already know what this feels like, allow yourself to experiment. Spend a few minutes leaning against one and sensing its presence. It might be easier than you imagine since these are powerful beings, maybe hundreds of years old, with roots that go deeply into the land, so their energy field, their spiritual presence, is in proportion to that. You don't have to get specific information for the experiment to work, just allow yourself to sense the quality in a wordless and feeling way. Notice what you notice.

There is a principle at work here. All life is there in the Field. All life. And much that you might not consider to be life. I would like to stretch your idea of what that might be with this story.

Dorothy Maclean was one of the founders of Findhorn, where they grew huge plants, herbs and flowers of dozens of kinds, most famously the legendary 40-pound cabbages, in what was originally the barren sandy soil of a caravan park in the challenging climate of Northern Scotland. Findhorn later developed into a large spiritually oriented community and training centre. The success with growing drew on her deep connection with nature and her ability to hear the "voices" of plants and the land, receiving their guidance for the garden[12]. She referred to the entities with which she had this intuitive dialogue as "Angels" and "Devas," regarding them as the overlighting spirits that might hold the developmental blueprint of a specific plant, but also operated at wider levels. The following passage is from an early encounter through attuning to a pretty pebble and becoming connected with the energy that she referred to as "The Cosmic Angel of Stone".

"Yes, I whom you have contacted am concerned with vastly more than your planet, for I contain or am connected with mineral life which exists in various stages throughout creation. Nature is full of

---

[12] Dorothy MacLean: To Hear the Angels Sing

paradox, in that, as you seek contact with what you consider a lower form of life, you in fact contact a more universal being. The human mind codifies and formulates, which is within its right and purpose, but forgets that all is one, that God is in all, and that the basic substance of life, which seems most devoid of sensitive consciousness, is held in its state of existence by its opposite, a vast consciousness, too vast for you to do more than sense its fringes and know that I extend beyond your imagination as yet. You realise, too, that dense matter is influenced in its make-up by stellar energies.

"It was the beauty of this particular stone which drew you to me. Beauty is of God, beauty is working out in all levels of life. Consciousness of beauty brings you into oneness, into any part of the universe. You are contained in it just as I seem to contain universes within myself. The more you appreciate beauty, the more you are linked universally. It is good to seek the life of it on high levels, for then your consciousness is expanded."

Bear in mind as you read this that intuitives "hear" messages through the medium of their own perceptual systems and language. The Deva is not speaking English but communicating a thought-form, so when she is heard to use the word "God", that may be the nearest available approximation for a concept meaning something different than yours or mine and received through our filters.

Remember also that the intent of this story is to present the widest possible perspective for the nature of the Information Field because this frames what is to come. If it stretches your belief system, please bear with me in what follows. The resources section will connect you with some other similar sources[13] which, as well as being remarkably consistent, deserve consideration based on their outcomes. If you are looking for evidence that this is not fantasy or illusion, that is where it would be found.

---

[13] Machelle Small Wright: Behaving as if the God in all of life mattered

In case you might think that the story above places our relationship with nature too much in a tree-hugger's frame of experience I would like to include here Harvard Emeritus Professor and double Pulitzer prize winner Edward O. Wilson. From the late 1970s he was involved in conservation, and some regard him as having created the concept of biodiversity. He also developed the science of sociobiology, where he proposed that the essential biological principles on which animal societies are based also apply to humans. He maintained that as little as ten percent of human behaviour is genetically induced, with the rest being attributable to the environment. In this he also prefigured both epigenetics and Spiral Dynamics as aspects of this book.

In 1984 he published his book "Biophilia: The human bond with other species." He defined *biophilia* as "the urge to affiliate with other forms of life". His argument for this is rich, drawing on the ways that humans use language to refer to nature and the pervasiveness of spiritual reverence for animals and nature in human cultures worldwide. Such spiritual experience and widespread affiliations with natural metaphors appear to be rooted in the evolutionary history of the human species, originating in eras when people lived in much closer contact with nature than most do today. It's one more arena for exploration.

What's in the land?

I would like to extend the notion that pebbles can be a small representation of a larger entity. I will draw again on a narration from Juliana[14]. For several years we lived together in a house with an acre of land. We cared for and developed that garden, which had beautiful pairs of old Yew trees and Scots Pines that stood like sentinels or guardians. My role was to dig and shift earth, with Juliana taking care of planting, all under the instruction of the plant spirits, but also of the land itself, not just our plot, but also its relationship within the local area. Alongside, she was developing her wider awareness of ways to work with the healing of the land and

---

[14] My former partner, as introduced in the opening chapter

with the spiritual aspects of places. With her wife Yvonne she now leads experiential tours held in that context. And they live near the Malvern Hills, which is the starting point for her narrative.

"When Yvonne and I came back from living in Pennsylvania we needed to choose where we would like to live. So, what is it that draws us to a place or repels us from another place? We could say logically well, it's, it's because of, you know, housing or population or whatever, and sometimes we don't have much choice. But when we have an open choice, isn't it really the energy of the land and the feel of a place that calls us?

I know that the Malvern Hills called me all those years ago when driving up to Wales. I saw that ridge and it was like - oh, there's something there. The first time Jon and I went there, when we had a caravan, I got out of the car in the supermarket car park and thought, Oh, I could live here. It was just that; that land and I had a good relationship.

Then other things develop about what the "beings" are and all that goes with that. Well, it's kind of interesting because, as I said, we were drawn to the Malvern Hills, and I always knew that there was a Dragon ridge there. The Dragons have imbued themselves into the land. I already knew that because I was asked to wake them up when we were driving around. I know that there's an absolute connection, that beings are connected to place.

It's hard to know what to say that's coherent to most people. We don't have words for it. When I say Dragons, it conjures pictures of winged lizards that breath fire. But that is an image of the power. Maybe that is what people felt and made stories of in the past. Perhaps they felt the heat, the fiery volcanic energy that is there underneath, the flow of the energy, the spirit that created it.

It's similar when we go to Ireland, Glendalough. It's a place where the High Elves live, and they come and talk to us when we go. They live in that particular area because it's a glacial valley with a clear lake. They always come across the lake in their boats, they live in the mountains. That's the way we see them. We've had that experience over and over, of beings in mountains. It's so normal for me and I don't know how to translate it for others. When you get elves in myths and stories it's because they are images of what was there before us, what originally created that environment.

Then, of course, the plant beings relate to the land. I say beings, but that is another way of describing a field of information, identifiable clusters, just as we are fields, collectives of associated information. This was a message that I received from an Olive tree in Greece that speaks to her relationship with the space."

"I am cast in a deep trough of this land. I drink the nectar of the bees, the soil and the substructure that allows me to distil liquid sunshine into my fruits and the oil produced from me. I am the first food of this land and I contribute to the gentle, strong energies here. As you drink my oil, you are rehydrated and rejuvenated. I give abundantly in accord with all I receive - there is a constant stream of give and receive that occurs as one impulse. Allow my strength to seep into your veins. Draw the sap of my oil deep into you and add to the gold of your own being. We, together, will create magic. Dance with the food of the gods - the olive and the bee nectar."

It's clearly different to experience the world around us in the way that Juliana describes. It's an embodied sensing practice that most of us don't have, although it is available to us all. Even to read her descriptions calls for a way of reading the words which sees through to the spirit within. The ordinary presentation which we are accustomed to leads us towards The Witcher, Middle Earth and elves as human-like creatures, with pointed ears. Here, the invitation is for us to engage with something more subtle that lives in the non-ordinary contexts. It connects us into a past and a folk soul of ancestral and mythologised non-ordinary awareness. It calls for us to go within and sense how this aspect of the unseen flows into our existence, even when we may not be noticing it. Whether you experience it or not, it is in you too; you might choose to discover that experiencing for yourself.

How we develop (and how we don't)

"The greatest discovery of my generation is that human beings can alter their lives by altering their attitudes of mind."

William James, The Energies of Men, 1907)

A while back we looked at our very early influences, many of which are invisible to us and difficult to investigate. As we get older, we take on language and acquire more explicit memories, making it easier to see and verbalise some of our own patterning. We also witness the way people around us are, and our memories at 10, 15 or 30 provide some data from which we can make better assumptions about our lives when we were 3.

Some important things happen in those early years. Foundations are laid for the people we will become. Our neurology changes and our capacities expand. There is a natural sequence to development which may be supported or inhibited by our experiences, particularly by the way we are parented.

I am about to describe that natural sequence, using as a basis the evolutionary model formulated 50 years ago by Prof. Clare W. Graves, which he based on his data about adults. Over the years Spiral Dynamics has expanded his theory. We can see that the sequence applies to children too and I have used this as the basis for a book on parenting.[15] Children go through identifiable stages, each of which needs a different way of parenting. How well we all adapt to those changing requirements affects who they become. So, we will look at this shaping process using the mirror of child-rearing.

As I describe the stages and associated needs, I encourage you to reflect on how your parents interacted with you, and what influence that has had on who you are now. I would expect some of them to

---

[15] 7-stage parenting: how to meet your child's changing needs.

be quite visible. This is not for you to be critical of them, nor of yourselves now if you are parents. It is merely to observe what is, and to provide an opportunity to reshape your responses. I acknowledge, though, that for some people, the reflections may be uncomfortable or even traumatic. There is a sliding scale of impact for both the actions of others and our responses to them. The resources list for this chapter may be helpful if you need to deal with any of the extremes.

Basic Graves/Spiral Dynamics

Simplifying this rich theory to its most basic level:-

> Humanity has evolved in stages by developing its priority codes for existence.
> We can operate from these stages as adults, and we prepare for them in our childhood.
> These codes exist as adaptive potentials within us which emerge if the conditions are right for them.

The priority codes in order of development, colour-coded for ease of reference are:-

	Colour	Keynote	Characteristics
1	Beige	Surviving	Food and water, safety and protection, procreation
2	Purple	Our "Tribe"	Ancestors and Kin, Security, Bonding, Roots
3	Red	Inner Identity	Empowerment, Developing Ego, Power over my world
4	Blue	Codes to live by	Learning the rules and becoming socialised
5	Orange	Outer Identity	Who will I be in the world and what will I create?

| 6 | Green | Human bond | Connection to others, fairness and care |
| 7 | Yellow | Integration | Health within each stage and balance/blend of 1 to 6 |

These abbreviated descriptions of the codes should make more sense as we explore the child's journey. However we will give more attention to the first four stages because they are early shapers of our lives which we are less conscious of. Later stages are more visible on the surface and easier for us to change through choice.

Beige: Parent as incubator

The first humans to evolve existed in small bands, as hunter-gatherers, without technology or settled agriculture. They were just one step up from chimpanzees. Their life conditions were very challenging. On a daily basis their needs were for food, water, shelter and safety from predators. So the primary Values and priorities for humans in those conditions are related to **survival** needs.

It does not take much imagination for us to see the newborn infant in this light. We are just about the most helpless newborn of any species, and certainly for the most extended period. Your baby depends on you for everything, and there is nothing else to be done but to take care of those needs. Keep them moderately warm and free from harm, feed when hungry, clean when soiled and comfort when distressed. It's as simple as that. In principle, anyway.

What can go wrong: the child who does not have this basic care may retain a deep and long-lasting sense of insecurity and always meet life with anxiety, distrust and caution.

Purple: Parent as Tribal Chief

Mere Beige survival was a raw existence. As humans became more skilled at it and numbers increased, conditions were created that made it possible to band together in larger groups for **safety and stability**. The possibility developed for a tribal existence, with wider relationships and greater security.

For the infant there is a gradual widening of their sphere of perception. At birth, her needs are immediate, all-consuming, and biological. As parent, you are an extension of herself; you are the part of her that meets those needs.

Some of this continues, even as she begins to crawl and to explore the world. The process of mastering the physical world is a long one for humans. A calf is walking within hours. We take a couple of years to develop the body size, the physical strength and the coordination that enable such a big brain to be transported upright on two legs.

Mastery of the environment is also about knowledge, but this is not intellectual understanding. Children are learning how life works, but this is a magical, mysterious experience. They spend a great deal of time watching and listening. They observe; they copy. They learn language. They tend to adopt their parents' habits and will love familiarity and routine.

In this stage, Mom and Dad are the tribal chief and shaman. They carry the wisdom of the tribe. This magical safety in a big and threatening world is a foundational element for healthy development. For a child at this stage, the family and its environment is the entire world, and that world is surrounded by mystical and magical beings – including Father Christmas and the tooth fairy. Psychological safety depends on these sources of security and a deep sense of bonding.

What can go wrong: Failure to bond and lack of a sense of secure psychological roots can be like an inner vacuum, a gap that can never be filled. Dr Gabor Mate has been a pioneer in exploring this area and we give some references to his publicly available material. He describes how a deficit in this area might be experienced as trauma and may lead to later conditions such as drug dependency. It may also be obvious that where failure or neglect create one set of conditions for damage, abuse will produce others. Whatever the child experiences at this stage of development may internalised as "this is what love looks like", so abused children may later choose abusive partners. Or they may become abusers themselves.

Thankfully, most of us are fortunate enough not to experience these extremes. But we are all shaped by the qualities of our early experience. These may mould our view of what males and females are like, or of what foods it is normal to eat and whether we eat together. You can explore what you may have taken on for yourself based on what you know of your family environment.

What do you think shaped you?

Red: Parent as Border Patrol

I once heard this definition of the stages in infancy.

1. Pre-crawl.

2. Crawling.

3. Walking.

4. Out of Control

Welcome to the Red stage in human development.

Stages don't disappear – they go within. Beige and Purple are our foundations; we don't stop being concerned with our personal survival, our desire for belonging remains strong and we never quite let go of Father Christmas. Even if we reject them, our parents live in us all our lives. But if you have heard of or experienced the "terrible twos", you have a fair notion of when Red starts. With most children, you'll know for sure when it kicks in. There are reasons too, why you should welcome it.

Being the same as our parents would limit us. New energies need to assert themselves because it is natural for us to be individuals and not just clones of others. For the developing infant it is essential and healthy that they begin to chart their course away from being the same as mom and dad, and start to find out who they are. They need to develop their sense of "I". This is often a strong life-force, **assertive and impulsive**. They feel the force of their own desires and emotions in an impulsive and raw way. "I want what I want and I want it NOW".

A child at this stage will begin to say "no" and "mine". Depending on their nature, this can go into full-scale resistance and tantrums where they lay kicking and screaming on the floor. There are several stages in child-rearing where the need for love is greatest exactly when you may feel it is least deserved. This is one of them.

Your child still has no ability to rationalise. You cannot persuade him out of a tantrum. However hard you try to tell him the reasons why, he cannot hear them. You have to wait for the emotions to pass.

This is a crucial stage. Finding ourselves as individuals and having the strength to be who we are will show up in every part of the life that follows. The only way that we do that is by trying things out. It's not conscious and is very impulsive. The journey is about what space can I create, what can I do and what can't I do? The strength of the emotions is hard for the child too. Beneath it is the danger, the underlying disquiet that they will break the bonds of security and lose the love. That is why love is needed more than ever.

In this stage we are finding where the boundaries are, and we can only do that by pushing them. This is why parents need to operate as border patrol. We have to hold those boundaries with firmness and care because however stubborn they are, however intensely they shout and scream, the developing self is vulnerable and potentially fragile.

What goes wrong: holding boundaries can go wrong in either direction, excessive firmness or lack of constraint. When parents are too rigid and punitive, the message to the child is that they don't have permission to be who they are. Their position in the world is to be without power such that any sense of personal purpose or reason to exist may fail to emerge, or do so only weakly. In contrast, when parents are too allowing, the message to the child is that they can have whatever they want, so they don't develop a balanced awareness of their place among others. While this can mean they will show up as a tyrant or bully, it can also mean that they feel abandoned and unsupported.

Our culture can often be disapproving of ego. But people need a healthy ego in order to be effective in the world. We need to distinguish between that healthy state of knowing that I am a valuable individual who has a reason for being here and the egotism of the person who thinks or behaves as if only they are important. When looking at what has shaped you, be conscious of the need to reflect on where you may be treating yourself as unimportant or not deserving of your place just as much as you critique any self-centredness or think you must put others first.

Where is that balance for you?

Blue: Parent as Rule-maker

Red, as just described, is not a comfortable stage. It is often turbulent and emotional, with all the potential vulnerability I described. The boundaries our parents give us may also be insufficient as we engage with a wider world of school, friends and society as a whole. It is not sustainable for every interaction to be a battleground and something with greater stability is needed. We need boundaries that are reliable and predictable.

This calls for **codes to live by**, structures that outlast individuals, secure means of trade and codes that keep neighbours at peace. In the larger context Blue stage coincides with written rules, legal codes and police enforcement, religious systems and priesthoods (Judaeo-Christian, Islamic), accounting and trading governance.

So it is with childhood. As the infant emerges from the turbulence of the Red years, it begins to re-awaken its curiosity about the collective. It is another swing from being about "I" toward questions of how "we" live together. Individual boundaries are not enough and there are containers for "my will". Her family is surrounded by something bigger. She may not have a concept of what society is, but she knows it is there.

Blue begins to emerge out of Red as the child develops a kind of pattern-recognition about the ways in which her impulses are responded to. Typically, society then takes on the role of codifying those patterns, particularly in school. There is a gradual process whereby she becomes socialised and accepts that there are generic codes about not taking someone else's toy, about not hitting, about one cookie each. The fairness of one cookie each may have been present from early on as an instinctive knowing. The codes are now being made more explicit, turning into rules.

Blue development is a long stage. It begins to be visible at the end of kindergarten and will last all the way to pre-puberty. Red impulsivity will continue to break through. Blue has some understanding of consequences; if I do X then Y will happen. To start with we may not be good at articulating this or at self-managing our responses. Gradually we are taking the external boundaries inside, and individuals vary a lot in how fast they can do this.

The Blue stage likes rules, and will become more attentive to consistency and to the need for reliable application. As it develops in us, there will be the beginnings of a wish to have explanations. Why is this decision different from that one? When we know what is right, we do not have to face either the public shame of getting it wrong or the subsequent internal guilt. There is comfort in the codes, and some people may live their entire lives with this as their priority.

What goes wrong: rules can block development by being be too rigid, unable to respond to changing conditions, allow no space for an individual to bring something new or be the person they are. If you want an example of the last of these, think of how intense the debate has been over the decriminalisation of homosexuality or the legalisation of same-sex marriage.

For you as an individual, you may well know what structure is behind the rules you grew up with – a religious system or a communist ideal. You will probably know which rules you came to reject, or where you have bent them in order to do what you needed to do, or suffered because you could not. Someone who grew up gay in the 1960's, or who was raised as a pacifist and then drafted into an army would have had to deal with such conflicts. But there may also be things that you hold without question as fundamentals of how to live. There is an opportunity here to notice what those are, and how they have made you you.

Orange: Parent as Manager

In the socio-historical development of humanity, the Orange stage is a relatively recent one, approximately 250 years in the West, and it is one that many countries of the world have not yet fully acquired.

The conditions that call forth Orange ways of thinking are formed in the limitations that Blue Values bring. The orderly Values of collective rules are challenged by the next stage of individualistic assertion, but this differs from Red's self-gratification and power-seeking because Orange individuality has Blue under its belt. Orange feels the Blue rules restricting its inventiveness, creativity and ability to bring forth the new. But it has also learned the rules.

The great positive value of Orange in human development is that it is an **inventive, creative surge**. In the individual this occurs as the teen years approach and the maturing child readies herself to find out who she truly is, and what she is here to do. The first thing that the teenager needs to invent is herself.

In order to do this she must distance herself from her parents. She will become focussed on her peer group, or on subsets of that group, possibly trying out a succession of identities in a compare and contrast exercise and there may be a generational element to that search, as a whole cohort of youth begins to set the agenda for their adulthood. Nature supports the process by creating surges of hormones that break down previously established order in the brain and body-mind. This may cause the teen to revisit any unfinished elements from Red such that Orange can sometimes look similar to it in behaviour.

You can look for yourself at what that was like for you. It can take many years to become clear on our adult identity and it may continue to evolve. You may recall a narrow path between not wanting your parents to be involved, while wanting and needing their support. If you are a parent you may see this from the other side and recognise why the role is increasingly hands-off and akin to being a manager. One question to ask at this stage concerns how the blend shows up between being shaped by the world and choosing for ourselves.

What do you see in yourself?

Green: Parent as Guide and Mentor

Green can arise in children quite close in time to Orange. As the child pulls away from parents, he looks for other ways to feel the support of others. At the same time, Green also arises because the Orange system in the outside world can be very materialistic. School may treat teens as numbers to be pushed through exams or be seen as soulless Blue authority that doesn't care.

	GRAVES VALUE SYSTEM			PARENTING & EDUCATION
Age Range (Approx. onset)	Mind-set	Capacities / Needs	Education Techniques	Poten
Birth to 1	Food, drink & shelter. Whatever it takes to survive.	Be taken care of	(Observation and pattern-sensing) Carer	Senso Devel
1-2+	Connecting to people and home, developing sense of trust and belonging	Role models	Let them copy. Story and myth Tribal Chiefs	Weak Attac
3+	Discovering identity, ego & self. Who am I?	Push boundaries	Guidance and repetition of action Border Patrol	- Lac + Exc
5+	Learning codes to live by; logic.	Develop basic logic and reasoning	Traditional teaching Repetition of explanation Rule-Maker / Enforcer	- Erro + Rig
13+	Mastering the world Strategies for life. Who can I be?	Complex reasoning and deeper analytical knowledge	Lead them into increasing self-directed experiential learning Support Experimentation Facilitator / Delegator	- Lac + Exc Limiti
15+	Mastering myself and what am I a part of. Who are we? Who will we be?	Seeks fairness and care Self-knowledge	Encourage group work, shared experiences Support exploration Mentor / Facilitator	- Lac + Exc Limiti

Development can become arrested at any stage. - or + indicate effects of deficit or excess

Note: All stages persist as new stages emerge. All boundaries should be treated as "fuzzy"
For educational approach, each technique should be seen as a building block that continues to hav

In this stage we can feel undernourished and hunger for more sense of human connection, to care and be cared for, to be part of a fair world, and to understand the inner nature of who we are. Green is looking for human **bonding**. Teens will often form cliques, and not necessarily in a nice way. For instance, while some girls are forming bitchy cliques obsessed with fashion there will be others who become strident in their humanitarianism, and extreme in their concerns for fairness and equality, often highly disapproving of those who do not comply. But within the choice and alongside their Orange individualistic focus runs a deep need for the security of a peer group.

What do you remember of this stage in your development? It is possible that you may have settled in Orange and that your career and achievement focus were dominant. However, the title of this book straddles Green and Orange perspectives. Orange is looking to be "the best me that I can be" and since that tends to call for some understanding of our inner worlds and to know what has shaped or is shaping us, it is likely that some Green orientation is part of the reason you are reading.

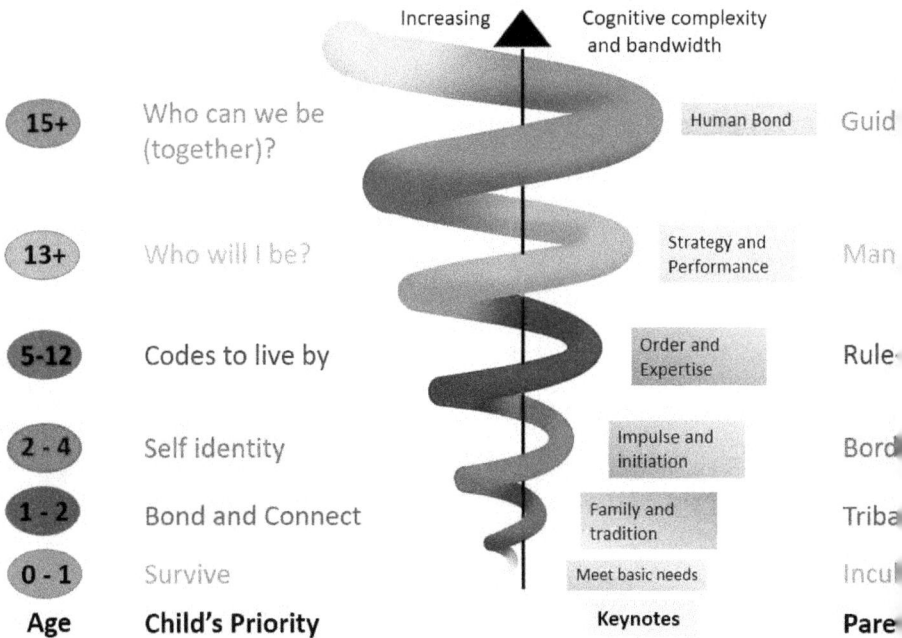

Increasing ▲ Cognitive complexity and bandwidth

Age	Child's Priority	Keynotes	Pare
15+	Who can we be (together)?	Human Bond	Guid
13+	Who will I be?	Strategy and Performance	Man
5-12	Codes to live by	Order and Expertise	Rule
2 - 4	Self identity	Impulse and initiation	Bord
1 - 2	Bond and Connect	Family and tradition	Triba
0 - 1	Survive	Meet basic needs	Incu

The Yellow Stage: Seeking integration

The diagram above does not describe the seventh stage, even though it is becoming increasingly important. But it is key to the journey of this book because seeing the many influences on who we are, including the contributions of stages Beige through Green, is a way to integrate the complexity of being human, spirit, body and mind.

What does it mean to be an adult? When do we become truly grown-up? I suspect that we all know people who have reached their 30's and more, but who are still behaving like children in some part of their lives, struggling with impulse control or unable to create order. Some even get to lead countries. You may recognise some aspect of this in yourself. I say this without criticism as I have witnessed it in myself over the decades and I hear it from my coaching clients. It's the human condition, bless us.

And what does it take to create a functioning world in today's conditions? I won't describe the problems we face. The diagram expands in a way that indicates the increase of complexity and perspective bandwidth through the spiral of development. To meet those conditions calls for the biggest adaptive shift that we have yet made. As Einstein said, "We cannot solve problems using the thinking that created them." Yellow priority codes are the entry point to our new thinking. More than ever, we must see whole systems. One core theme of this book is that you are a whole system. What does it take for you to see all of you?

There's more still to come, so read on!

Understanding Mindsets

A change of worldview can change the world viewed.

Joseph Chilton Pearce, The crack in the cosmic egg.

As you have probably noticed, we don't all think the same! But as for what creates those differences, there are so many factors that this chapter could easily take hundreds of pages. I will address just a few of them.

There are plenty of theories of personality, some of them quite rich and potentially useful, but with a few exceptions, personality is something that you just have. It defines you. You may be able to emphasise the good parts and hold back the rest, but it doesn't change, and that limits its value. Let's just acknowledge that we all have personalities and move on. In fact, anything that is not open to you making changes is of low significance for this book. I will focus instead on what has shaped our collectives, and on the process by which we individually emerge from those backgrounds.

Cultures

Culture is quite a broad term with several potential layers or scales. There are the larger features such as the nation that you grew up in and the identity which that fostered. Most of us also grow up in neighbourhoods or perhaps extended family environments which also deliver their own perspectives on life. Nowadays culture also includes all that bombards us from social media and TV. In some respects this is homogenising humanity with global brands like Coca Cola and Manchester City Football Club. I recall being in Bali in 2012 where young men knew the names of many UK soccer players.

While much of the above has the benefits of bringing forward the thoughts and life wisdom of our grandparents, or creating new shared entertainments, it also brings prejudices and entrenches historical enmities. My ex-patriot South African friend with Boer ancestry recently spoke to me of how the scars of a war that is now well beyond 100 years in the past still affect relationships between people who could be the ages of her and my grandchildren. The English are still the enemy.

If you have grown up in a family of migrants, you might have experienced how such cultures create a feeling of home by still cooking their traditional foods. Many cities have specialist shops for Chinese, Indian or Polish ingredients, offering vegetables that I don't know the names of. While that is on the surface, not far beneath are ways of thinking that developed in different places, different political systems and different climates. Your family may have had expectations of what job you would have, how you treat your grandparents, and who you should marry. Traditions are persistent, some of them, like honour killings, regarded as completely out of step with modern life. They are still the stuff of newspaper headlines and TV dramas alike.

For many of us, such family and neighbourhood expectations are our "normal". We may be accepting and tolerant of differences, but they don't vanish. Your normal and my normal are not the same. It was always this way, even before multiculturalism, because there were regions in countries, villagers and city-dwellers, ruling and lower classes.

Every element in this list of variations might contribute to "who you are". Maybe you have thought about this in relation to your own being, maybe not. If you have, you might easily see these as definitions, external labels such as my knowing that I am (approximately) a white, middle-class, professional British male. But while those descriptions will have influenced me and affected who I am seen to be, they say very little about who I really am. How much have you thought about how these influences have shaped who you are and how you see the world, and what frames the choices you make? If you haven't, I encourage you to spend some time observing your thoughts, what you say, and how you respond.

Take a little time to question "where did that come from?". For every thought you have, there is the potential question "is this mine?"

How many of the things you believe are yours, and how many have been handed down to you, swallowed by you along with your family breakfast or passively absorbed from influencers, media personalities and politicians? If they are not yours, what might happen if you let them go, mentally return them like an unwanted birthday gift?

Religions

In the previous section you might easily have wondered why I didn't mention religion. Of course, there is quite an overlap between religion and culture. Despite that and in some ways even because of it, I see it as worthy of a distinct strand of enquiry.

Some years ago I listened to the good-humoured dispute between two friends, both of them atheists, over which of them had been programmed with more guilt by their respective backgrounds in Catholicism and Judaism. They could have that debate because both of them felt that in some measure they were "over it". In the background there remained a powerful sense of how they had felt affected or even damaged by their experiences.

I use this example to illustrate the perspective that it can seem as if religions are about what we believe and therefore that we can simply change our minds about that. I would like to show how far from the truth that is. There is an expression from the Jesuits "give me the child until he is seven and I will show you the man". I see that as true, even though millions have lapsed from whatever faith was pushed on them.

Some people I know who have a spiritual faith have a standard response to someone who says "I don't believe in God", which is to ask, "what kind of God is it that you don't believe in?" One of them would even add "Maybe I don't believe in that God either." This is a useful question for believers and unbelievers alike.

Religions are not only about what God is, though. That would be too easy. It is said that if you picture God as the moon, religions are fingers pointing to it. Whatever God is, when we talk about religions, we are talking about the various fingers and how they are pointing. More than that, behind each finger you can imagine humans, each of whom is looking in their own way through their own glasses and filters. Each of them has a preconception about what the moon is – whether it is made of cheese or has a smiley face.

Each religion interprets the Divine in its own way. They are as different as Buddhism[16] and Catholicism, Judaism and Jainism. They all have their own view of how we should live. In most cases they have sets of rules that they perceive God to have laid down for us to follow or obey, and priesthoods whose task it is to interpret and maybe enforce them.

So, what did you grow up with? The answer has probably shaped your view of God, what it is you do or don't believe in, whether you have a soul, whether that soul had a before-life and will have a life after death, and whether or how you might be held to account for your choices in this life.

We are shaped not only by what we believe and align with, but by what we reject. That is to say, your mother may have told you some things about life that you now follow and comply with. Equally you may have rejected what she said and be determined to rebel and not to follow. In either case, she established some criteria and boundaries, and those are part of the shaping container for your existence until and unless you set yourself completely free of them. Your attitude to God and to whatever you have been told are God's requirements and expectations operate similarly. Supposing you have ever done personal work to set yourself free of such programming, whether from your family or from priesthoods, you know that getting free of all conditioning can be hard and can take a long time. If you have not done that kind of work, it is not my intention to push you in that direction; it is your choice to discern what will or will not increase your happiness. However, I suggest

---

[16] Close enough to a religion for these purposes

that developing some awareness of what is there can have great value.

As with culturally supplied thoughts, if you haven't already, I encourage you to spend some time observing what you say and how you respond to events or ideas. The earlier question applies: "Where did that come from?". For every viewpoint you have there is the potential question "is this mine?" One of the strongest elements in most religions is that they define what is right and what is wrong. The rules are often absolutes; the tablets of stone are in our heads.

I have a favourite quotation which comes from Mark Twain – "It ain't what you don't know that gets you into trouble, it's what you know for certain that just ain't so." One of the themes of this book, as we reveal just how many layers there are to our existence, is that certainties are in very short supply, rarer than we might think, and for sure rarer than others tend to assert. The world is inherently paradoxical, and it is without question complex and changeable. It is a living system and our responses to situations ultimately depend on context. There are times when simple rules don't work. Even the Dalai Lama acknowledges that the rule against killing is not an absolute; there are times when it can be necessary to prevent even greater harm. He couches this view within the context that you must be willing to take on the karmic accountability for the act. In a living system, yesterday's best choice may show up as tomorrow's worst.

Moral philosophers can and do tie our heads in knots over such challenges. For each of us the question concerns who we choose to be in difficult situations. With the theme of this book being "What makes you you?", what happens in this arena is that we are each operating in the space between the rules handed to us, the personal or more general principles that those rules carry, and our own ways of making choices. And where this overlaps into culture is that many of those rules or principles have become embedded there. We have cultural contexts about the value of work, about freedom of expression, about how much money it is OK to have, about who should or shouldn't have sex with each other, about who cares for Grandma, and how. Those contexts may be filled with differences of opinion. Still, many of them are suffused with points of view that originated in religion – the protestant work ethic, the apostle Paul's view of marriage and chastity, the difference between Christian and Islamic views about charging interest on loans.

Ultimately, I suggest that the factors mentioned above collectively influence what makes you who you are. The challenge, the task for each of us who cares to be conscious about what we do, is to be as aware as possible of the mindsets that are in operation and to make our decisions accordingly.

How conscious can you become?

Education

Jesuitical thinking extends beyond the realm of religion as well. That you are even reading or listening to this book probably means that you went through schooling, possibly including kindergarten. Society gets its hands on you and your mind, and it too has an agenda. For this section I will focus on primary education, the ages up to 10 or 11.

Once again there is wide variety in what you get. There may be a national curriculum. There may be an educational philosophy to how that is applied, and whatever there is at those levels may be augmented, undermined or even ignored by any school or teacher.

What was your early schooling like?

In theory, education is about teaching you skills and facts. Can you read, write and do arithmetic? Do you know the water cycle or the difference between mammals and reptiles? In the background is a developmental process involving behaviour, learning to listen and interact, and developing self-discipline. This is the essentially universal human journey of living with others without conflict, managing the instincts and impulses that we inherited through our evolution from apes and pre-language hominids. That takes time, and in theory such an education would get us a long way in life. It could be relatively benign, allowing us to learn from and about the world without any distorting agenda. It would teach you how to think, not what to think.

Theory is one thing. Real life is another. What most of us get is a training, not only in what to think, but in what questions to ask, or not to ask. Sometimes this is by deliberate intention to instil a political or religion-backed "right way"; some questions may not even be permitted. Sometimes the training rests on shared views about how the world works. It is unlikely in either instance that you were actively encouraged to challenge convention. I doubt that what you were presented with was even framed as anything other than "this is reality". We praise the Einsteins who look with greater curiosity at what might be real, but we rarely nurture them.

What was your experience and what's your worldview? How much of it was fed to you by this kind of system? How much of it was contrary to what you felt or knew inside? This book has already introduced some concepts such as constellations that don't fit with the reality we are taught. I know people, and maybe you are like them or know others who are, who were sensitive, intuitive, psychic or aware as children. What they knew and experienced was not acceptable; they were told not to make up stories and soon learned to silence their inner knowing or at least not to share it.

There are degrees of this, and when we get to later education there will be more for us to explore regarding the difference between the concepts that have been presented to us and any alternatives that are more accurate and less limiting. Depending on your experience, I repeat the encouragement to examine what you have been told, what you already know from your own experience and awareness, and where the discrepancies are between the ordinary presentation of reality and the many phenomena that don't seem to fit.

Develop a habit of checking in with your deeper knowing and asking, "Is this my truth?" Notice where you are sceptical about alternatives and unconventional points of view. Where are you willing or unwilling to open up a wider frame of understanding? What are your certainties, and can you be sure they are reliable?

All that I am presenting in this chapter has arisen from my own journey. I was once a conventional thinker, and I have learned the hard way over many years not only that the world is stranger than I thought, but that it is stranger than I even know how to think. More and stronger evidence of this non-ordinary reality shows up every year. That which has made you who you are so far is less than what can make you who you will be in the future. It's an opportunity, and we have a long way still to go.

Contexts

"We are shaped by the particular soil, climate, history, and psyche of the place in which we are born."

James Hillman, *The Soul's Code*, 1996)

Our mindsets, as generated by many influences including those in the previous chapter, are also framed by our relationships to a variety of contexts. However much you may feel like a consistent centre in your own existence, you adapt to where you are, who you are with and to the types of interaction that pertain to those different environments. Are you the same person with your family as at work, or do you show different aspects of your being? Different histories have shaped those spaces, different expectations are operating, and you probably make different choices about what information you reveal or how you display or suppress your emotions.

Place

Where did you grow up? Did you form a relationship with that specific territory? Or maybe with places that have a similar character. As I said earlier, for myself, I know that growing up in the foothills of the Mendips made a difference to me. I am drawn to other parts of England that are like it. Flat areas somehow leave me feeling likewise, even though I know that they too are beautiful, and other people wouldn't want to be anywhere else. I am proof that you can take the boy out of the hills, but you can't take the hills out of the boy.

Does it make a difference to our existence to live in a desert, or by the sea? What does that question mean to you? I referred to the two years I spent in Arizona, feeling that my soul was parched, and not because of the heat. Maybe there's a deeper genetic history, an instinct that knows this will not be an easy place to find food or water and yearns for a greener environment. At the same time, I know that people grow to love places that I wouldn't, and to feel a part of them. That includes cities, because there are people who would not want to leave London or New York.

You may also be open to the idea that places themselves have spirit, sometimes referred to as a *Genius Loci*. This is certainly how the world is perceived by shamanistic cultures where people may engage quite directly with the spirits that animate local flora and fauna, in addition to whatever they perceive as the creative force for their particular environment, their forest or their prairie. But other cultures have this concept too, including the Romans, who originated that Latin phrase and who set up altars to honour the presence of protective spirits.

Nowadays when we may have access to foods from across the globe it is easy to forget that there was a time when most of our nourishment came from that soil and the creatures that live there. Eating grubs and insects is something that we may watch with revulsion on "I'm a Celebrity" but that is part of normal diet for others. Likewise, the lighter skull and jaw that you have in comparison to the shape of Neanderthal ancestors reflect the cultural development of cooking, without which meat, and many vegetables too, would be tougher than we can manage. This is what it has taken for us to be taller than they were and to walk fully erect.

Whatever your diet, your body has likely adapted to it, even when it may not be a healthy one. It has become part of your context. When you remember that our biological purpose is to survive for long enough to produce the next generation, the long-term damage of processed food doesn't matter. The push for health, the worry about obesity or heart disease is driven partly from survival instincts, but also from cultural expectations or the societal implications around health care, and even from our attitudes to death and dying. To some people none of that health conversation is important.

In fact, your body itself carries the history of past environments. This is more than the obvious feature of skin colour or hair; Inuit are short and squat because that shape reduced heat loss and was suited to climates that are always cold. While these typologies have been diluted over millennia, there will be features of your physiology that may contain traces of genetic resistance to diseases and conditions that your ancestors were dealing with 10,000 years ago. The context that you live in now may not be fully aligned with those origins. Some of my ancestral roots were in the Middle East; I notice that in every English winter.

However, most of our contexts show up in the content of daily life rather than in our physical surroundings. While some of them overlap with culture, much of what follows affects many countries, most strongly the developed world, but if that is not where you are, you will be able to generalise what I say to your own location.

Secondary Education

I see two relevant aspects to how education shapes us. However much governments and teachers might like to pretend otherwise, school is not only about developing knowledge and skills. To the extent that it is those things, there are many questions about how successful it is at that. Was yours? Either way, school is also about fitting people for society and employment, and about "socialising" them, moulding them and their beliefs about their world to the shape that is seen to be required. Alongside that, it is a place where we learn how to manage our relationships with others outside of our own friendship groups. Some might also say that it is a place to confine adolescents while they go through their challenges so as to minimise the harm to the wider world. As Eliot inquires in "ET", how would you explain school to a higher intelligence?

I won't go further into that theme, except to invite you to consider what effect it had on you. You are the expert on that. In particular I acknowledge that responses may vary considerably by age as well as location. There are new generations which receive so much online and via social media as to make formal education less relevant. If that applies to you, please take that into account. But we are all put into school, and my invitation is made on the basis that it is very easy to take it for granted and not to think about its effects. It's just there. So, my suggestion is that you set aside the curriculum and list the 3-5 other most significant things that school taught you, and maybe consider whether they turned out to have value for your life since. In what ways have they made you who you are? And what ways of your being are despite school or even from intentional rejection of it?

The second aspect is deeper, and concerns the nature of the world itself. While very varied, there is one thing that is fundamental to most educational systems, and this becomes more relevant when pupils are above 10 years old. We live in a scientific and technological age and an emphasis on the scientific view of reality is to be expected. However, it is essential to recognise that many aspects of what this book presents do not operate within the scientific worldview, a theme to which we will return regularly.

Conventional science lacks a context for understanding spiritual experiences or the worldview of shamanistic cultures described above. Science as presented in our educational system aligns with what is also current in our media. Anything that is not operating in the material realm does not have a place. The result is that many centuries of human experience are treated as irrational. Even in countries that teach religion, there is no connection between a curriculum for faith or spirituality and one for science. This creates an environment where it is difficult for individuals to have both.

If you have had any kind of experience that does not fit within the explanations offered by material science, it is likely to be regarded as non-rational. Technically, to be intuitive, or psychic, to "see a ghost" or feel the presence of spirits in nature, or to have a mystical experience such as an epiphany or knowing the nature of "oneness", is labelled a form of psychosis. It is seen from a scientific perspective as an accident of humans having evolved complex and imaginative brains. There is nothing about it that can possibly be real.

The effect of this education is to marginalise those who do have such experiences. It is to undermine the basis on which religions exist by placing all belief in God in a realm of psychological comfort blankets. All healing methodologies are rejected, including some like acupuncture with millennia of systemic understanding behind them, and others like homeopathy with a few hundred years of practical evidence and a very scientific methodology. The "placebo effect" is built into the protocol of all drug trials without any understanding of how or why it works.[17]

How this affects you will depend on what you have experienced and on how strongly the conventional view has persuaded you. You might be comfortable in that space and have a sceptical perspective on what I am saying. However for many individuals the outcome is to feel silenced and dismissed. The impact on research is substantial and this may have prevented you from receiving the benefits of other health perspectives.

When it comes to anything like spiritual experience, conventional education restricts us to talking about that in psychological terms rather than as a fully valid aspect of the real world. At the interface between spirituality and healing sit a wide variety of valid approaches to well-being. In a world that likes to talk about holism, our education makes that hard to achieve. I regard it as certain that the split between science and spirituality is a significant contribution to the widespread crisis in mental health and workplace stress. Beneath all of that is a mechanistic view of what it is to be a human being, and we are paying the price for that – a price which includes massive actual costs in antidepressant prescriptions and the like.

Economics

A now-legendary sign in Bill Clinton's campaign headquarters read "it's the economy, stupid!" No-one who has been part of a Western electorate will be shocked by that; the majority of people vote with their wallets. Are you typical of that majority? Is money important to you?

---

[17] The Science of Possibility – see note i

It is not easy to say "no" to that for a simple reason; we associate money with our survival. The thought of having less brings up fear. Few people are immune to that. Even if it is not our physical survival that is at stake, we all have dreams and ambitions, for ourselves and for our loved ones, which feel like part of our psychological survival.

I used "economics" rather than "money" as the heading for this section because how we think and feel about money is embedded in the system that we are part of. I will assume for the purposes of this narrative that you are reading this as someone living in the system known as "capitalism" and it is not my purpose here to debate the rights and wrongs of the various expressions of that concept. Rather, I wish to talk about where it has come from and how it interacts with the ways that we think and behave.

In an earlier book[18] I explored the nature of our relationship with money in some depth because money is not merely something mechanical, even if economists might sometimes present it in that way with "laws" like supply-and-demand, or political debates about debt levels, growth and interest rates. The "market" and the "invisible hand" are (systemically flawed) concepts that attempt to lump us all together, but in order to examine this context, we need to get personal as well. What is money to you?

I am taking us into a somewhat circular argument here, because how we feel about money is written into the system we have built, such that it isn't mechanical at all. The dynamics are deeply emotional. They express our fear of lack; our fear of losing what we have; our desires, acquisitiveness and greed; our relationship with power and how we might use money to express power in the world. They express the human desire for control, how we can use money to influence and manipulate others or to shield us against an unpredictable world.

Each of these elements inhabits the way that money works such that it is not merely about what capitalism is, but about what kind of

---

[18] Reinventing Capitalism: How we broke money and how we fix it, from inside and out

capitalism we are operating. One big problem with money is that we have come to believe that if we can manage the money, we are managing life itself. This is a myth, and the world is currently in a state that demonstrates how flawed a belief that is. We are failing at a planetary level, and we are failing at a human level too.

I do not regard that as a political statement but as a statement of fact, though since politics and economics are connected, we will address politics shortly. The system is the shape it is because people with power set it up to support them to preserve that power. They are still the ones with hands on the levers. It is set up to support disparities in wealth because that was seen as the appropriate reward for creativity and entrepreneurship. It is set up to see you and me as economic units. It is set up to treat corporate entities as independent from society and environment so that they are not required to do anything about their effects in those areas. It is set up to prioritise competition over collaboration. In nature there is a systemic balance between those forces which has made evolutionary development possible. Nature doesn't systemically outsource side-effects. Our economies are the shape of past human thinking as created by those with power and control.

How any of that shapes you personally may reflect your place and history in the system. It may say something about your moral priorities and underlying values. Once again, I am encouraging some contemplation. What is your point of view and where does it come from? How do you see the presence of fear of loss, fear of lack, power and disempowerment, desire for stuff, using money to control yourself/life/others, to be showing up in your system? What is it about life that has contributed to becoming the way that you are? These are major questions, and they are worthy of deeper examination, particularly if you want to make more aware choices or if you feel that the current ways are not working.

Following on from that, what features of the current economic system do you wish to see change? Here we will transition into politics, because while some of the features of the system are built in structurally, for instance having corporate entities accountable for money but not society or environment, some of those features might be shifted by legislation. Beneath these questions are some fundamental attitudes to how life works. Suppose you believe that survival is a battle, a fight to the death, that produces a different perspective on what is needed when compared with the understanding of ecosystems, where all participant entities are in an emerging dance of co-development that balances competition for resources with sharing for mutual benefit. As said above, our systems were developed in eras that had their roots in the former perspective, and competition remains a strong mindset. Living systems perspectives and mycelial networks[19] are more recent developments. How you see the world will blend these perspectives with your emotional responses. I find, and you may too, that this places some of my life choices in tension.

Politics

Does this heading make your heart sing? Mine, not so much, less and less with every year. How much does your government represent your view of the world, and how many of its policies do you actually approve of?

As with the rest of this chapter, the challenge is to delve beneath the debates to examine our core question. Like it or not, our political context shapes us. I have a friend who was in a Hungarian prison during the Communist era for challenging the system. Living in the UK after being in several other countries over the decades, he is still not a Communist. But he is an ardent proponent of social, communitarian and alternative economic approaches. The egalitarian ideal is in his bones.

In the West, we are quite likely to think that democracy is the best way to live. You probably take it for granted that this includes women's right to vote, because that was already accepted in most countries by the time you were born. One hundred years earlier you would have grown up with different assumptions – maybe agreeing

---

[19] Entangled Life: Merlin Sheldrake

with the system as it was then, maybe resenting it, maybe simply accepting it as the way things are.

But maybe you didn't grow up in the West or even in a place with a meaningful vote? You might be from Zimbabwe or Russia, or other countries where elections have been completely rigged. So how do you think society should work? Does socialised medicine seem like a good idea? Who should care for the elderly?

I am reminded of a story about a man who was asked the secret of his 60-year marriage. He said, "That is simple, I make all the big decisions, and my wife makes all the small decisions." This provoked some shock, and further explanation. "My wife decided where we should live, how the children were to be educated and where we went on holiday. I decided our policy on nuclear disarmament."

Besides recognising how this illustrates that big or small are matters of perspective, it asks something about how we are shaped by our political context. You might not have had a choice about educational systems. If your country didn't have nuclear weapons, disarmament would not have even been a question. How aware are you of the context that shaped you, and what you may have never questioned, and which nevertheless inhabits your choices now, even your voting intentions? It is not so long since it was normal for most people to have lifelong affiliations to the point of identification. "I am a Republican/Democrat, and all my family have always voted Republican/Democrat." How many different parties have you voted for during your life? What shaped your choosing?

In all these contexts, we can see ourselves as the product of various types of relationship. Outside me are my family culture, my social environment, my economic and political surroundings. There is me, there are those contexts and there is a third entity in-between, which is the ongoing relationship between me and the context. That relationship has a life of its own, a blend of the changes taking place either side. I have some agency and can partly shape what happens in that relational space if I am conscious about doing so. Still, there is much that I cannot change and must adapt myself to, and yet more where I am probably not even aware that my current choice is a default that it has never even occurred to me to question. What are the questions that you have never asked, and what difference might it make if you were to ask them now?

Connection

"Intuition is a method of knowing which goes beyond intellectual analysis; it grasps the absolute in a direct experience."
Henri Bergson, *An Introduction to Metaphysics*

What do I mean by this chapter title? Connection to what?

In the last chapter I described how our education in a mechanistic model of the universe, where spiritual experience is viewed as irrational, naïve and scientifically ignorant, has sent the half of humanity that has such awareness into the closet.

Maybe that applies to you, and maybe it doesn't. Even if it isn't you, the question of how you view the world and what you believe to be "real" is still in the frame. I remind you again of the question that some people like to ask of atheists - "What kind of God is it that you don't believe in?" But it is just as significant for the religious, the faithful, the believers, the "spiritual but not religious".

I am going to offer my own perspective, which I see as offering a new way to address many of the arguments and seemingly incompatible points of view. It is a way to make both science and spiritual experience equally valid and real. And whatever your take on its rights and wrongs, it provides a different screen onto which you can project your own views and choose your identity. Our experiences in this realm, or the absence of them, also make us who we are.

What does intuition mean to you? What about being psychic or clairvoyant? Have you ever known what someone was about to say or had a person come into your thoughts minutes before they phoned you? It is not so unusual but often discounted as coincidence or accident. My perspective starts there.

I introduced my personal journey with this scientific enquiry by describing a profound experience of precise psychic knowing, created under witnessed and quite well-controlled conditions. I was obliged to recognise that I had just done something that my scientific upbringing said was not possible and that my rationalist mind-set could not compute[20]. It brought a profound shift that has underpinned decades of exploration, providing the frame for the inside-out view of reality that I am offering you.

I remind you now, in that experience I was able to detect an aspect of someone's body – someone of whom I had no previous knowledge and who was apparently 100 miles away. He was merely "David" a name on a card that someone else was holding. Yet I was able to make a connection to him and feel something of his experience as if, for that moment, I was him. In that instant of link-up I experienced the discomfort of his brain tumour as if it were mine and asked if that was what was written on the card. It was.

I was impelled to explore this phenomenon because I don't believe in magic. By that I mean that I didn't stop being a scientist, and I view the seemingly magical only as something about which our knowledge is not yet adequate. Therefore, I treated it as a certainty that there must be an explanation for how it was possible. I needed to understand the universe differently. Further experiences or witnessings followed on a regular basis, such that there was no alternative for me but to seek an expanded scientific model for the universe that would embrace the old one.

Realise what always was

When Galileo and Copernicus demonstrated that our planet orbits the Sun, the Earth did not change. When Magellan circumnavigated it and proved that it was a globe, the Earth did not change. The famous "blue marble" picture taken from Apollo 17 didn't change it either; it simply changed how we saw it and how we saw ourselves. We realised what had always been, and those realisations have been transformational, maybe not instantly, but certainly over time. The first changed religious power and authority structures. The second removed limitations to our boundaries and the third opened us up to see a new connectedness, the dawn of a one-world, one-humanity perspective. What is the next expansion?

---

[20] I describe this event in more detail in a Substack post

Today's conventional scientific picture is merely another mindset. Many humans view our world as only matter, also believing that we have mastered significant elements of it. Some of us have embraced Einstein's insight that matter is energy made into form, but only as a theory. $E=MC^2$ is a mathematical construct rather than what we see every day. A few may know a little about quantum reality and entangled particles, even if we can't grasp that. These too are descriptions of what was always there but not seen. After so many centuries we might have been expected to learn how much less we know than we imagine we know, but it seems to be difficult. Perhaps we crave the comfort of a certainty even while at a deeper level we feel unsafe because we know it doesn't exist.

What have we still not seen? Are you willing to step across that difficulty and into the next realisation of what has always been? What might that bring? What might it enable and empower that raises our capacity to deal with the challenges we face? That might be worthy of some effort to stretch ourselves.

Creating God in a human image

Human history has witnessed similar shifts in its perspective on what might lie beyond us. We had a view that God was a kind of tribal ancestor, one that resembled us, looked and felt as we do, but with more power and wisdom. To some extent we have gotten over that and perhaps we know somewhere that Michelangelo's old man in the sky isn't real, yet it has been hard to escape that personification, that father-figure who might punish us, and whom we pray will intervene to stop the wars and punish whoever we see as an evil-doer. It will help us if we can shift out of that and stop projecting human ways of thinking onto the Divine. It would be helpful if we owned our own rules and principles of behaviour, beyond the limits of stone tablets.

A more recent historical trend came with materialist science which brought with it a full-on atheistic rejection of anything resembling a Divine presence. Science doesn't have an ecosystem for God to live in because it allows nothing outside of matter and nothing outside of you or me. In its view, there is nothing between us either, except for feelings or emotions. There's nothing real, nothing to actually connect us, only figments of our imagination. The only spirit that materialism allows, is human spirit, and it doesn't seem to think much of that either.

The Blue Marble supports a sense of our shared participation in something larger. That has become associated with a transcendent, sometimes mystical, experiential sense of connectedness. The reality presented from that frame is oneness; there is no separation, and to the extent that God is a relevant concept, we all live in that. But we only live there in spirit, because the material rest is illusion, the Hindu "maya", imagination from our egos, which are false. It is the polar opposite of materialist science.

While that has an underlying truth regarding the nature of the cosmos as a single energetic entity and the all-pervading connection at the quantum level, it has always felt unhelpful to me as a human trying to live a life of meaning in my biological form. There were no questions arising in day-to-day existence either at a personal or collective level, to which it delivered useful answers. It is a chocolate teapot, at best ornamental, and at worst dangerous when filled with boiling water. Oneness is similarly unhelpful when crossing a busy street. We need differentiation, the boundary between I and Not-I.

Shaping energy into form

It is time for something more. Knowing that matter is made from energy is also a truth, but it similarly misses the point. What shapes energy into form? Perhaps an answer to that question might lead somewhere useful, and indeed it does. It enables us to realise something powerful that always was, but which we haven't seen yet. It is our next expansion.

There have been clues to that answer offered by past awareness of the akashic field and by the much more recent theory of morphogenetic fields put forward by Rupert Sheldrake. Fields are indeed a significant part of the picture, but these are examples of a more general feature of the universe. I want us to revisit some thoughts that I introduced in the first chapters.

That general feature calls for us to turn all that we have thought upside down, or perhaps inside out. I am inviting you to see Information Fields, cosmic consciousness, the spiritual realms and intuitive awareness alike as demonstrations of this reality. All of creation is shaped by what the Universe knows, the record of everything that it has brought into being, throughout its existence, from its first moment until now. Let me try to describe how that has worked, and how it continues to operate now.

Omniscience

In its first moments, the Universe of energy created zillions of forms, most of which were unable to sustain for more than tiny amounts of time, but a few of which were viable, robust and sustainable. These were the building blocks of a material universe, quarks, protons, electrons and the like. Over a longer period, these units coalesced and formed larger structures, including atoms and molecules, stars, and galaxies - the fabric of the cosmos as we know it.

In order to do that, to replicate initial sustainable structures over time and on a cosmic scale, the Universe had to have had a way of "remembering" its blueprints. More than that, it had to hold the knowledge of what it had created down to the level of every particle and the relationships between them. When physicists speak now of quantum entanglement, the connection is informational. There is an expression taken from Matthew's gospel (10:29-31) which says that God is aware of every sparrow that falls, "And the very hairs on your head are all numbered." Detailed as this sounds, it is crude by comparison when the field of information is aware of every particle of every molecule in every cell of the sparrow's body.

The Information Field does that because it continued to retain its recording as elements and molecules became organic, creating amino acids and proteins, evolving into cells and multicelled organisms, and eventually into you and me. The processes of life continue the self-creating activity by which the universe has developed increasing complexity and continues still to do so. It is never-ending. It is the nature of life as we know it.

Omnipresent organic divinity

The Field is everywhere. Please don't view what I am describing as some kind of exterior, or as disconnected and observing us from a distance. There is no distance. The Field is in everything, present through everything, and connected in its knowledge of it all. Since life developed in that organic manner, creating its increasing richness, the information is located within. It is part of matter and connects all of it. It is omnipresent. **It IS the oneness**.

Among the results of that, the Universe, the Field of Information, knows precisely who you are. Yet it isn't personal in any human sense. It has the record of everything that is and everything that has happened on the way. In that sense St. Matthew was accurate. But what I am describing here is a cosmic science, the laws of creation which are the way they are because that is what happened. It isn't an exterior design; rather it is a self-created outcome, an emergent evolutionary result in which the processes themselves are God's law. It is an organic divinity.

This makes it essential that we don't think of God like a super-powered human. Earlier, when I described our historical views, they were all projections of ourselves and our earthly relationships. That was understandable for people who lived in a rainforest or were only familiar with a world that was 50 miles wide. Even when humanity's worldview expanded to one that included awareness of other nations, it was not totally irrational to project our power onto the Sun or to wish to appease Thor and avoid being struck by a thunderbolt. It was conceivable to think of God as residing in the clouds, waiting for us to join him as angels with harps.

None of those stages in our view of spirit come close to what is needed for today's humanity, knowing as we do that Earth is a speck among billions of galaxies. Star Trek and Dune may be fiction, but it is only a slight stretch for us to believe that such things as travel between worlds are possible. Instead of projecting human-scale thinking onto spirit or the Divine, we are now called to find our place in an order that has a vastly different scale of cosmic consciousness, not just bigger than we ever imagined but bigger than we are even capable of imagining now.

This delivers us a remarkable mixture of something vast with something quite intimate. Your own interior[21] Information Field is primarily concerned with you and what or who is near you. I use the word 'near' in either in the sense of spatial proximity or in regard to your daily concerns and the people you are connected with and who are connected with you. Your awareness and thinking are part of the field. This is a matter of what you are in relationship with, such that the nearness is of a very different dimension than even that of your nation, let alone our solar system or the cosmos. Similarly, it is intimate in the sense that the field's connection to you is also relatively local. To put it another way, the influence is stronger where the field concerns you in particular.

What's the connection?

For phenomena like my psychic detection of David's tumour to be possible, there had to be a feature of the universe that connected my awareness to him. That feature was quite specific in enabling me to locate him individually in a country of millions on a planet of billions. It was without any limits in space because it would have been the same if he had been thousands of miles away. The connection that took place was wide-band and qualitative; it wasn't a single data point but an experienced stream of felt-sensing. I knew the nature of his pain as if it were my own.

I would like you to have a sense of what that takes because that is key to grasping the nature and the power of the Information Field, or Knowing Field as it was in that moment. You might have seen references to quantum entanglement, the scientifically proven fact that two tiny particles can be connected across huge distances such that a change to one is instantly associated with a change in

---

[21] Allowing for the fact that interior vs exterior have a fuzzy meaning in this context, where all boundaries are porous

the other. While that is significant as proof that informational connectedness is real, it is infinitesimal when compared with what I am describing, where the field encompasses everything that is.

The Field is a master description of the entire universe, down to the state of every atom and cell within it. If you want a "mind of God", that would be it, the creator before form. At the same time, it is all accessible to us, and we can shape aspects of its unfolding because we hold, or we are, a portion of the field. As a result, you can choose what to connect with, just as I chose to connect with David. Please pause for a moment to reflect on how powerful this is.

I mean stop. Think about it.

You are a receiver for everything in the Information Field, with built-in addressing mechanisms that no one understands yet, but which work in practice. If there are limits, no one knows what they are, so there is a very, very big space for us to expand into. Merely having that awareness of everything is potentially transformative to what human beings are and to who you or I are. I invite you to breathe into the magnitude of that.

Awakening from the mystery

In one sense, it is a mystery due to the newness of the concepts. Yet once again, this is about realising what always was. The frame I am presenting does not alter the nature of reality regarding what the universe is or has always been, but it should change how we perceive it. It provides a multitude of possible responses to the fundamental and age-old human questions about who we are and why we are here. There is also a great deal of data about how humans have experienced this non-material realm. It can be found throughout the centuries in reports of mystical experiences and myriad stories of psychic, shamanistic and non-ordinary phenomena. It is in the Vedas and the Tao Te Ching.

I use the term data because, despite the vast amount and how it comes from every kind of human in all kinds of cultures, it is not "evidence" in terms that our current scientific method would allow. In my book "The Science of Possibility[22]" I laid out in detail the many ways in which the data is present around the edges of what science has shown and is willing to accept. However, I am not trying to drum up readership. You don't need it; it's there for the curious and those who want more backup. Instead, you only have to open your mind to a new way of seeing. The Earth always orbited the Sun, it was always a globe and it has always been an organic, connected whole, the outworking of an entire realm of connection. The Information Field opens a new way to understand how that connectedness works. Once seen, it cannot be unseen. If you are looking for a mechanism that makes sense of how constellations or in-utero experiences, or astrological influences might work, then here it is, if you choose to embrace it.

So where do you stand?

Thus, I come back to the question of what kind of God, or Divinity, or Universe you believe in. Or don't. Some of the implications of my perspective will show up again later, though you don't have to accept them either. Throughout this book the question is one for you and your choice of who to be. Now that you have seen more of the influences on that process, you have an opportunity to choose what you will take from them, which conclusions you now see to have been handed down to you like a family recipe for sponge cake, and which ones you wish to keep. Maybe you prefer fruit cake or chocolate brownies anyway. Again, every belief that you have, every thought that runs through your mind can be subject to the question "Is this mine"? If you sense that it isn't, then you can let go of it and choose something different. It's your life. It is up to you what and whom you connect with.

This leads into our next chapters, where we will look at some of the implications for models of the world - material, non-material, psychological and spiritual with the intention of broadening our

---

22   https://www.amazon.co.uk/Science-Possibility-Jon-Freeman/dp/0956010733

perspectives on who we can be and what we might do. Ultimately, all that we have explored in respect of what has made you the you that you are now is a preparation for expanding our views of who we can become and how we make changes.

I hope that you find that thought exciting.

Models and Maps

'It is a beautiful thing to connect the stars to our biology, because that's what we are in this fractal universe – beings of passion, made from the stones, the stars and the minerals of the living earth.'

Richard Rudd

This narrative has been building a multi-faceted and multi-layered perspective of what it is to be a human being. Bit by bit we have explored what it is to be incarnated, present in a place that lies between spirit and materiality, being both soul and mind, shaped by external influences and interior choices. The picture that we have built has numerous ways to expand your life, merely by delving deeper into the elements that you choose.

You don't need a model. However, there are many models and maps available, and you may find one or more of them helpful and supportive as you navigate the territory of your existence. We must always remember that the map is not the territory. The <u>territory is always the master</u>, is always richer and more complex than any map, and changes faster than any map possibly can. In our context, you are the territory and therefore you are the master. So never think of fitting yourself to the map.

Allow me to extend the image a little further. You can draw many different kinds of maps for a geographical space. You might only draw a map of roads and centres of population. Typically that is enough to navigate a cross-country drive. If you were hiking you might want a map with contours so that you could see where the steep hills are, and you might want it to show rivers to follow and crossing points. I could go on - with administrative/political maps so that you don't cross a border to somewhere you wouldn't like to be, or with weather maps showing annual rainfall. The point of this is to understand that maps have their own purpose which will shape what you see and how you see it. The following are a few maps that

I suggest are effective in helping you see and navigate all that is being presented here.

I am choosing models offering elements of the dimensionality that this book is covering and that convey the possibility of development in the many facets of human existence we are exploring.

The Kaballah

The Kaballah is a rich and ancient system for spiritual understanding, most strongly associated with Judaic mysticism, but with diverse roots in Assyria, in Greek mysticism, in Hermetic principles and most recently in Theosophy. I don't claim any expertise in it, but I know people for whom it is rich enough to be a lifetime study. It also has many ways of interpretation, such that the labels in the diagram are single-word simplifications of complex and nuanced ideas, and in some cases, I have chosen my own words in order to highlight a few elements of what it conveys. Nevertheless, I see those elements as having great importance.

The first key feature of this model is in the trajectory from the top circle, which represents the Universe itself, the Field of Information and which I have called "Divine Flow", to the bottom circle, the manifest, representing conventional material existence. The nine circles in between represent aspects of you as a human individual and as a body operating between the universe and earthly existence. I believe it is helpful for us to always have in mind the way in which we are physically located within the knowing field.

Secondly, it presents a relationship between different aspects of your existence, the relationship between the three triangles of your cognitive functions, your emotions and your embodiment, the last of these being facets that are located in more instinctual aspects of your Being. In my presentation the Field connects to every aspect of you and thus is not as external as this diagram might imply. Each of the circles represents an aspect of your relationship with your world and an internal place from which you relate.

In a similar way, when viewed vertically, the diagram represents three pillars of these relationships. On the right in this presentation are the archetypes that represent judgment and a more Yang orientation to existence, whereas the left is more Yin, more merciful and forbearing. In the middle is balance. Thus all of the ways in which you might see yourself reflected in aspects of the Kaballah offer different possible views of the spaces in which you relate to the world. Taken together, they provide a great deal of flexibility in how you might orient yourself.

One last sidebar about the Kaballah. This book raises many questions – even if only implicitly - about the boundaries to human creative possibilities. Our individual ability to influence the Field operates within the independent unfolding of the Field itself, and alongside the creative contribution of other "actors" who may not be only our fellow humans, but any other conscious entities, whatever you may conceive those to be.

There is an age-old consideration of "my will" vs "God's will" because the belief is widespread that humans have been given free will and that God is not micro-managing our Earthly existence, still less the unfolding of the entire cosmos. This comes most strongly into focus around our birth and death. Some of what has been said previously about soul contracts, together with astrological and Genekeys profiles might be seen to suggest that we have choice over our birth times. That would require some degree of coordination with others in the field, most obviously our mothers, but ultimately the field as a whole has to cooperate.

What then of our time of death? We live in a society that believes strongly in the postponement of death and in the potential for medical intervention, or even first-aid resuscitation, to bring people back from the borders of death. We have defibrillator machines in public places. I understand that as few as 5% of people are successfully revived in these ways once the heart has stopped, but first responders and ambulance crews make a great effort to prevent that from happening.

There are some whose interpretation of the Kaballah is that our time of death is predetermined to the same degree as our birth because other aspects of the wider flow depend on that. Might that be true? It makes sense at one level in terms of the co-creative aspect of soul contracts, our agreements with others. Consider the impact on family dynamics, inheritance, corporate succession or political events as just a few of the ways in which other people's life plans or soul trajectories may depend not only on when we die, but how and

TREE OF LIFE

INTELLECT   EMOTION   INSTINCT

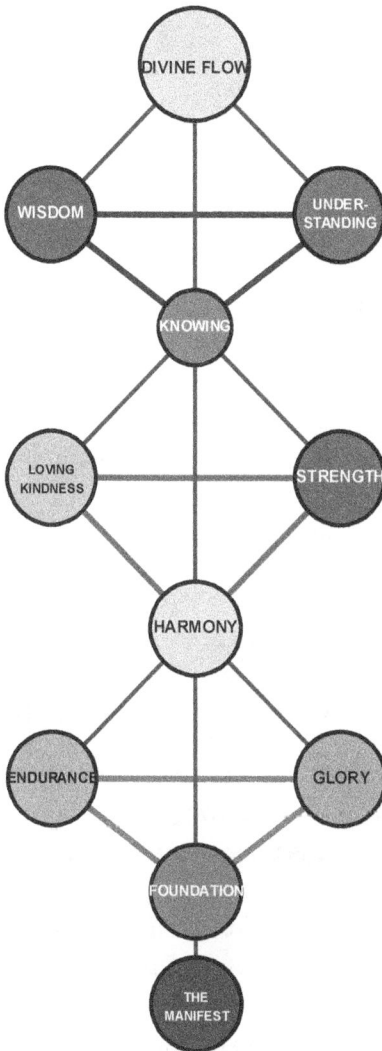

where. The question for those with spiritual belief regarding "whose will?" contrasts with the randomness of events in the scientific materialist frame. How much freedom to choose do we have? I don't know, though I have a preference for the thought that whatever we might have planned just becomes an option once we are here. As generals have said, "No battle plan survives contact with the enemy". In any event I am very aware that the blend of randomness and contractual choices in the flow of the universe itself would be impacted by how that works.

Astrology

Astrology is an ancient system which has been misunderstood, trivialised and misrepresented.

My friend Pam Gregory has written a book "You don't believe in Astrology, do you?" I recommend it highly, as I do her YouTube channel because Pam is one of the most scientific, logical and analytically detailed people I have ever met. Yet her choice of title goes to the heart of the question, because on the face of it, astrology is easy to present as complete bunkum. I would like you to look at it from a very different perspective.

As in other areas of this book, I invite you to turn the usual perspective inside-out. What is on the surface is very different from what is underneath. What does astrology look like if you put the Information Field first, and the material world second?

The obvious and seemingly devastating scientific view of astrology is that the zodiac is a fabrication. Astronomically this is undeniable. When we look at constellations such as Aries or Sagittarius, we are viewing the star map in two dimensions and only from here on Earth. The view from the surface of Mercury would look very different, and in both cases the stars we are looking at may be many light-years away from each other if only we could see the depth of the visual field. There is no connection between them, so nothing to exert a collective influence on you or me.

I should also dispense here with newspaper star-sign astrology which is subject to the equally obvious charge that it is ridiculous to suggest that one person in twelve will have the same experience today as all their fellow Pisceans. But that is not astrology, which is complex. Your chart is as unique as you are. Nor is anything predetermined; we are talking about influences in the flow.

Yet I am saying that I do "believe" in astrology and that is because when done correctly and with detailed understanding, it works. Pam's book provides a lot of evidence, and I also see it as consistent in producing accurate profiles for myself and people that I know. How can that possibly be so?

Belief has nothing to do with it. I don't believe in gravity even though I cannot see it. Belief is irrelevant, since I don't float in the air even if I stop[23], and that is because there are laws and principles at work. Those laws and principles are operating in ways that we cannot see, just as the field around a magnet, which makes shapes from patterns of iron filings or orients a compass needle, is also only visible through its effects.

To make astrology work you must put the Information Field first. And then you have to embrace the way that humans detect the Information Field, seeing it as equally real to the way a compass needle detects the Earth's magnetosphere. In addition, you need to see how human consciousness operates, and with what depth of individual and collective awareness.

Have you ever been moved by a painting or by a piece of music? As I write, Daniil Trifonov is filling my ears with Brahms' piano transcription of Bach's Chaconne, played with the left hand only. It is filled with illusion, chords arising from notes that cannot be played together, melodies that arise from the ability to emphasise one sequence in the midst of many, and above all, emotions that are produced because my brain interprets the whole in its own particular way – but with similarities to other humans who also respond, just as Daniil and Brahms have done and that we assume that Bach intended. If another piece of music had been playing, and no matter if it were Miles Davis or the Eagles, there would be a similar story. If you are more visual, you can translate this to

---

[23] It is of course, theoretically possible that my mind could intentionally work to locally contravene or bend that law.

114 - What Makes You YOU?

Guernica or the Mona Lisa. Millions of us respond to shared messages. That is how the arts work.

We humans relate to our world through story. We make meaning of our experience. The word "bus" will immediately bring a small story to your mind, a form of transport larger than a car, carrying multiple passengers and with a particular image that has come from your context – a Red London double-decker for me – perhaps a yellow school bus if you are American.

I am still talking about astrology. The shared human narrative is filled with stories and myths. People have sensed things about the characteristics of what is in our sky and have made up stories about them. The constellation of Aries exists not because the stars are connected, but because people who were sensing their environment projected what they felt to be present in that portion of the sky onto the patterns that they could see.

Some of the patterns are very old and very deep. The Greeks and the Romans saw the planets as Gods and detected something energetic about Mars, Venus and Mercury that came to be part of our shared human history, at least in the West. All the characteristics ascribed to the zodiac and planets, down to the naming of dwarf planets, have arisen in this way. That which is known about people and about the interactions between these energetic entities, these patterns of information, the squares, oppositions and trines, has been developed from the experience of working with them and observing correlations. Is this science? Not if science means controlled experimentation and replication, it isn't. But it is scientific in the way that it depends on multiple observations, checked by different people and cross-correlated. And it is scientific in its method of looking at a pattern now and comparing it with a previous occurrence of the same configuration. One just has to bear in mind that the same alignment may have last occurred 12, 30 or 200 years ago. Everything I am saying depends on putting the Information Field first, along with the acceptance that humans can detect this information and that we have always done so.

Even when so much data is assembled and correlated, and even when you have a personal chart from a truly skilled professional, how you relate to it remains a choice, one that operates according to your own awareness of yourself and the events in your life. I would love to be able to offer simple answers here, ones that you can have delivered to you without needing to develop deeper awareness. But that is not how the alternative reality works. Nor is it the message of this book, which you will by now have recognised is layered and multi-faceted. Who you are is the result of many complex processes in the body and mind, all of them informed by the contexts of the relevant fields. Astrology, and our relationship with the movements of our "local" cosmos is just one more of those contexts.

Once again, I must also emphasise that astrology is another map, and what it has to say about you as an individual or about us as human collectives is not deterministic. Your birth chart doesn't tell you who you are, it is no more predictive than a hand of cards dealt to you in bridge or poker. It is what you have to work with, but how you play the cards is where the action is. As before, the map shows the shape of the territory. Where you travel, and whether you go on foot, by car or by bus, is up to you.

Genekeys

Astrology is an ancient study and another such is the pattern of hexagrams developed in China, possibly as many as 6000 years ago, and given their textual descriptions around 1000 years BCE. Again, we are dealing with a system that was developed by people who sensed patterns, just as they did with the patterns of energy in the body, the lines of chi energy that became the basis for acupuncture treatment. Some of acupuncture's knowledge can be validated by scientific detection, and its treatment results can be assessed against those of Western medicine. We cannot do the same   for   the   I   Ching.

If you have read the I Ching, particularly in translations which retain the imagery and language of its origins, you would recognise that we are again in the realm of stories. As with astrology, we are engaging with more profound mysteries and with invisible patterns. There are many ways to work with the 64 hexagrams, and a popular one is to use them as a tool for divination, getting insight into what may be present in the field at this moment and using that to reflect on what may be the next best steps and choices.

The hexagrams also form an annual pattern, with each of the 64 being present for approximately 5 days during the year. They represent fundamental patterns of unfolding in a cycle from beginning to end, spring to winter, birth to death. As with astrology we are engaged with a mystery that can be sensed but not seen, and as with astrology, the patterns of influence are present at the time of our incarnation and birth. They too, shape who we are, or the hand we are dealt. They too are an aspect of the Information Field, as real as electromagnetism, as real as the mathematics that determine how electrons are formed and how they orbit the nucleus of an atom.

It's ALL a mystery

I should emphasise, for the benefit of readers who may still be struggling with the desire for something more scientifically certain, that science is just as fundamentally mysterious. I have referred to magnetic fields, saying that no one knows what they are, but it's yet more than that. I have referred to gravity, and no one can tell you why that exists. They can predict a lot about it, and how its attraction relates to the mass of objects. They can tell you that attraction happens and predict its influences, but they can't tell you why. Nor can they tell you why movements of copper wire across a magnetic field cause electrons to flow and create electricity. It is ALL mysterious. Life IS mysterious. Our challenge is not that the worldview laid out in this book is a bigger mystery than what lies beneath our scientific theories. The challenge is that we have spent significantly more time, effort and money investigating the material perspective. We don't know what it might yield if we were similarly determined, patient and systematic in pulling together all these other, non-material systems and discovering the deeper truths of the non-ordinary reality.

Returning to Genekeys, this is a system that combines the patterns of astrology with the patterns of the 64 hexagrams to produce a rich metasystem. Building on the original insights of Ra Uruhu, Richard Rudd has enriched and developed the concept. I include it here because it works for me in a way that is even more uncanny than astrology and I encourage you to explore what insights it may hold for you.

I was tempted to include astrology and Genekeys in the early chapters because it would have fitted quite easily into the context of what we are born with, and our early shapers. I have chosen instead to place them in the context of maps and models for two reasons. One is that the influences are ongoing. They are with you now. The other is to draw us more deeply into the nature of the field itself, into the way that we need to look at what is real through our stories and meaning-making. More than that, I hope that you will be getting a sense of the way that what we don't know, what we might intuitively sense, what our bodies can detect and what our right hemisphere functions can find in the patterns, are where this other reality is unfolding before our very inner eyes - if only we would open them.

What would that take? Can we open them? We will go there soon but on the way, I want to take a little detour into the world of belief and experience to explore how the relationship between you and all that is around you works, so that we see more about where creation takes place. We are opening the door from what has made you you, into what will make the future you the one you choose to be.

The Enneagram

I am not sufficiently knowledgeable about the Enneagram to write well about it, and I would rather not take up space doing it poorly. However, I don't want to leave it out entirely as I have experienced its depth and respect the basis it has in Jungian psychology. I have put a couple of links in the resource section and recommend it to you if it pings your curiosity.

Beliefs and Experiences

"You can't say A is made of B or vice versa. All mass is interaction."

Richard Feynman. Nobel Prize-winning physicist

We are beginning a transition from your past into your future. We have touched on many aspects of the way that your perspectives have been shaped and what sits beneath or inside the way that your identity and views of the world have been formed. You are already Being the result of that. Our focus is shifting towards what and who you are Becoming.

What comes next takes place in the arena of your interaction with the world's own flow. What is already shaping up in that exterior reality? Then, since the Information Field is also in you and therefore shaped by your choices, you affect that flow.

It is far from obvious how that works. The formulation I have presented is new and not widely familiar. A few people have indicated its existence, but only in quite vague ways. Alternative and spiritual thinkers have played around its edges, seeing the effects but not understanding them. As said earlier there is a wealth of data about spiritual experience. How can we bring that wide and scattered spectrum into coherence so that it feels real and usable?

As an attempt to do that I would like to present some of those viewpoints, many of which you may already have encountered, or even tried to live by. I want to set up some connections so that the relationship between information, energy and material existence is more explicit. In particular, I would like to bring it closer to our bodies and the fabric of our being, as indicated by the many facets we have already explored.

The New Age: Law of Attraction, Positive Thinking and The Secret

If new-age and new-thought ways of working were fully effective, we would all be rich, in perfect relationships and constant bliss. So why aren't we? Whilst I want to acknowledge that many teachers and writers in that genre have done honest and sometimes brilliant work, and many healers and coaches have helped their clients, I see it as obvious that something more is required. Maybe something less in the way of ego, too. I feel as if we have been offered the Model T Ford with the sales pitch for a Lamborghini. That doesn't mean that all such automobiles should be written off, only that we have a lot more technological and usage development to do. Right now, we don't know how to drive this reality. What if we could do better?

I am in favour of empowerment and of the perception that we are more than we have thought ourselves to be. Yet we are obliged to deal with the paradox that while I am AT the centre of my Universe that doesn't mean I AM the centre of the Universe. It is true that when we unlock our internal barriers and release old thought patterns, it makes a difference. I received benefit from many approaches of this kind over the decades. Hypnotherapy, Havening, EFT among many available modalities can accelerate progress. Even so, The Law of Attraction would have us believe that by BEING the quality that we wish to see in our world, we will attract everything in the world that is resonant with that quality. If only it could be so simple.

Beware too, of the miracle stories. Remember that if 1000 people practice a particular technique, one of them is likely to produce the desired outcome, regardless of that practice. Sometimes, someone gets lucky. Most of the people who buy lottery tickets don't win. Millions of people read "Think and Grow Rich", and it is filled with useful guidance that has made it the number one book ever in this genre. Many people will have lived better lives as a result, but I suggest that the main people to get really rich were Napoleon Hill and his many emulators.

Regardless of these warnings though, there is an underlying truth to the law of attraction because we have creative agency through being part of the Information Field, so why is success still relatively rare? I will offer two suggestions.

1) BEING a frequency of prosperity, or of perfect romantic partnership is not easy. You are more than your thoughts. BEING is not something that you can do only with your mind. To the extent that it is your mind, it is not only your conscious mind. Such beingness is a product of your spirit, your soul, your body AND both your conscious and your unconscious minds. You cannot override any aspect of that collective that forms your existence merely by thinking it. Belief is not enough. Faith is not enough. With regret, I have to say that the Field responds to all that you are, not just the bits you want it to. Anything else leads to spiritual bypassing.

Your body and your subconscious are always switched on and engaged with the Field. Every fear, every tension, every shadow is active even when you are not thinking about them. They are creating attractor energies for the Universe to respond to. Your conscious mind is only on when you are actively engaging it on the topic you wish to attract. The rest of the time, it is busy doing other things, making breakfast, being at work, watching TV, fantasising about romance or sex or whatever might be the case for you.

You can't suppress or bypass what is real. A few people achieve remarkable results with intense belief and visualisations. True as those stories may be, everything useful that has been written about this area, every hero's journey, carries the message that we must face into our fears, discomforts and weaknesses. We must embrace them. They can only be transformed through acceptance and through love, loving ourselves with them, loving them as parts of who we have been. Only then can we release them and move on. Only then does their energy cease to resonate. Only then does our frequency change. Often this takes time because several of the layers of existence described in this book are involved. You must be willing to peel away the layers of the metaphorical onion.

Until that happens, stop pretending and fantasising. Work on the principle that the Universe responds to the lowest common denominator of your thought field and that coherence is increased bit by bit. Each incremental step has value, so be willing to celebrate the smaller "wins". Journey before Destination[24].

2) We are not in charge, but neither should we view this process passively. Our agency has boundaries, but we are also interactive with our world and with the wider sphere of creation.

A while back, speaking of contexts, I said "Outside me are my family culture, my social environment, my economic and political surroundings. There is me, there are those contexts, and there is a third entity in between, which is the ongoing relationship between me and the context."

This is not difficult, but it may seem to be so because our habitual thinking is so different, and that is what gets us into trouble. We get trapped in the polarisation between identity and oneness, between the illusion of separation and the presented-as-superior view that we are always connected at the level of spirit or consciousness. There is the Dual and the Non-Dual, where the latter is presented as a spiritually more enlightened perspective that we should aim to hold. It seems like an either-or.

We likewise get caught between humanness and divinity. As observed earlier, we project our view of the Divine outwards from our perceptions of what a more powerful, knowing, or wise being could be. We have always fallen a long way short. Even though our understanding of the cosmos has expanded, our ordinary conceptions of God remain very close to Earth and to us. That has made it easy to treat God like a person and to represent spirit as something or someone other than us, even though we may know that we are spirit too.

In a sense, Non-duality is non-existence, at least for you as you. Buckminster Fuller put it this way - Universe is by definition One. That's the "Uni" piece. And then within the One, there is definition or differentiation. There is I and there is Not-I, both creating. Both

_____

[24] Brandon Sanderson "The Way of Kings".

are real. Both are perspectives that you can adopt. So where do attraction or creation take place?

The answer is that they take place in **relationship**. They take place in the interaction between you (your own field of consciousness) and the exteriors that affect your life. Those exteriors can be at every level, in every aspect of the Field that you are engaged with, from your family and your partner to the national economy. The consciousness, the field that is "not-I" has its own flow, its own life, its own dynamics. When you step into the river you alter its flow, but it is still a river. You are always in relationship with your contexts.

What can you do: How do we get this to be real?

I repeat, you affect the flow. What does it take to enter fully into the relational space? How do we get ourselves out of the passive stance towards our own creative capacity?

Conceptually, the reality that I am offering you is really, really simple, as straightforward as flicking the light switch. That is a choice. You can make it, or you can walk away. It's a red pill or blue pill moment. The matrix that we have all been living in is, so far as I know, not a computer simulation. It's the Information Field.

Simple does not necessarily mean easy. My experience has been that the habits of thought and language are very persistent. In presenting the many aspects of your existence as I have done throughout this book, you have been hearing that you are more complex than you realised. Maybe a lot more complex. Even if you don't accept all those influences in the way that I have suggested, I imagine that you have taken some of them on board and that not all were previously familiar to you. I hope that your perception of the richness of who you are has expanded.

At the same time, I have invited you to turn our previous perceptions inside out. The defining feature of conventional frameworks for reality and for consciousness has been the degree of their orientation towards what is material, solid and tangible. They are what is real, and all that is in the world of spirit, consciousness and information is not. That is the nonsense that most of us were given.

How many films or dramas have you watched where one person doesn't say what they feel, where a message doesn't get passed on, where a letter is lost or hidden for years with the consequence that another person makes a tragic choice? It's the plot of Romeo and Juliet, described as star-crossed lovers, but ultimately just poorly informed. Information has consequences. How often does the drama arise from a statement overheard and taken out of its context, or facts and events being misconstrued or lied about? That is the plot of Othello.

That need for information applies just as much beyond the realm of human drama. The inbuilt laws of creation are the way they are, because Universe knows the laws. Humans have learned what some of those laws are and made use of them. Birds fly under their own power and humans have learned about aerodynamics to create planes, rockets and helicopters. But you can't take a bird or a helicopter into space because they need atmosphere. Rockets take us to the moon and beyond. We must apply our knowledge in a manner that suits the context.

The laws of information are just as real and just as important as anything that you see in the material world. The material world was constructed according to some of the laws of information. $E=MC^2$ is a phenomenally powerful understanding, but much less so than the laws that govern the shapes that energy takes when it becomes matter. Information is the shaper and the connector.

We aren't trained or educated to be information-aware. Often it is quite the reverse – if you have that kind of awareness as a child, it will get shut down. For much of my life I would have said that I never had it, but thinking back now, I can recall a time when as a five-year-old I spent several weeks with some kind of intense past-life memory of being in the trenches during WW1. I made a bunker at the bottom of my bedclothes where my teddy bear and I fought the enemy. At that age I had never heard of the trenches. We didn't yet own a TV, not that there was much to see on them in 1956. That experience lasted for many nights, though I have rarely thought of it since. But I have known other people who, as young children, had much more awareness. The one who was aware of the spirits of the past inhabitants of their house, the one who knew that this wasn't their first time in a human body, the one who always knew she had come from somewhere else besides Earth.

I told the story of my psychic awakening but I didn't say that I went on to teach the Silva course that had brought it about. I saw others awaken their "other" sensing – maybe less dramatically, but enough to know that they knew. Since then I have known without doubt that we all have the capacity within us. I have wondered what our society would be like if we were raised to know that reality and not to doubt it. Maybe you already know that, but if you are among the majority who don't, consider what life would be like if you had that information awareness and trusted it the way you trust your eyesight? Can you imagine that? What would it be like if millions of us did?

People are broadcasting all the time, or at least their fields are emanating. I believe strongly that we know intuitively when we are being lied to. Our problem is that we override that knowing. That is why people find themselves in abusive and dysfunctional relationships, and why they vote for scumbags and sociopaths. We have a weakness for gaslighting, and many of us will question our own sanity before doubting someone else. Indeed, it is now more apparent than ever that people will vote for serial liars when the message is the one that they want to hear. I like to envision a world in which the majority are aware that this does not lead to good outcomes and develop the self-esteem and awareness to respond differently.

Feeling the flow

The Universe doesn't broadcast, or even leak. Rather, it is transparent. Everything is in the open. The Field is the shaper and connector, and it is dynamic. It has to be, because otherwise life would stop and become inert. The laws of physical entropy don't apply here; life has continually increased its complexity and the amount of information it holds. It is not running down; instead, it is continually creating. More importantly, we, the human collective, together with other living things, are making choices, or at least taking actions, on a continuous basis. The plant which takes nutrients and sunlight and turns them into something we can eat, is affecting both the physical world and the Information Field[25]. All life participates in that co-creative activity.

There is no boundary between you and the field, just as there is no boundary between you and TV signals. TV stations are filling the airwaves whether or not you have an aerial or your receiver is turned on, and regardless of whether you are tuned to their channel. We all have a receiver for the Field, or perhaps it would be better to say that we all ARE receivers for the field - not only your mind, but your body. Our whole form resonates to it. The receiver is always in operation, but we are tuned to our 5-sense channels and only pay attention to those. My psychic story happened because my full attention was focused for that minute in a single direction. Still, we can also keep our general awareness open, just the way that you can take in a scenic view or focus on a particular feature in the distance. You know how to use your attention in that way with regular senses. You don't even need to think about it. The same is possible for your intuitive awareness. It merely requires that you create the space in your existence for it to operate.

Our transmitter is always in operation too. The field is hearing us the whole time. So, when it comes to Law of Attraction, positive thinking and all of that, what we create is typically coming from all the chaos inside, the unconscious, the habitual, the embodied patterns. They are all there like a kind of noise, an interference on the line. An engineer would talk about the "signal-to-noise ratio". If you want to be a coherent creator, you need to clean up the signal. That requires being more aware of what the noise is and where it is

---

[25] That is not to say that the information field doesn't also apply to rocks, only that they are less dynamic. Renowned for that, you might say.

coming from, which can be any of the sources in previous chapters, and some more besides. This book is not oriented towards that, and the blessing of the new-age movement is that there are thousands of books and toolkits. I mention a few in the resources section.

The relational space: What use is a wheel?

I said above that attraction and creation take place via relationship, in the interaction between you and things that are exterior to you. Let me expand on that a little to see if I can make it more concrete. In the Field, the boundary between interior and exterior is porous, but your sense of material existence operates in a different and more bounded way. You feel as if you are solid. The challenge to our sensing systems arises from that and from our perception of it. Bear with me as I come at this a little sideways.

It is common to see references to the wheel as mankind's first and greatest invention. That's a big mistake. I invite you to think of ways to use a wheel on its own. You could roll it downhill or use it as a garden ornament or perhaps play a game. In fact, it's not much use at all.

The axle is a much greater invention. When you have an axle, you can put it through the wheel. You can connect a container to both ends of the axle. Then you have a wheelbarrow. Better still, you can attach a wheel to each end, so the axle is positioned between them, which gives you something wider and more usable. You can put something on top of the axle and pull or push it from one place to another. You have the makings of a chariot or a handcart, or can even attach it to a donkey to carry a larger load. That is progress.

What's my point here? This is about Relational Being. A wheel is an object. A nicely shaped and even aesthetically pleasing object perhaps, but nevertheless only an object.

An axle, on the other hand, is an invitation to relationship. It can bring two wheels together or connect your barrow to the single wheel. It occupies the space between a wheel and something else and makes if functional. It is the beginning of a system, and systems are collections of relationships. Two axles connected to each other form a chassis, which provides you with four wheels that can support a horizontally stable structure. That is the foundation of automobiles and lorries, scalable to the size of an eighteen-wheeler. Literally and metaphorically, relationships and systems can take you a long way.

There's a principle here. If you have any inclination to see what I have said as trivial, I encourage you to look wider and deeper. Your life is not a bunch of wheels but a set of axles. You probably see a lot of people, most of whom are unknown to you. But when you connect with one of them you make an axle, which might be called friendship, or relationship or commerce. The friendship is a thing in its own right and you can even refer to it as a separate entity. Our friendship, our marriage. Where you have thought of those as being dyadic, with two people involved, there is in fact a triad.

Something exists in-between you and your partner. You can work on "our relationship". Without "our relationship" you are two separate people. The relationship is where the action is. This principle extends to all areas of life. In commerce, it is an agreement or a contract, both in what might be written down and in the interactions from which it originates. <u>Life happens in the connection between things.</u> There is little life in the things themselves. If you think of yourself as a thing, please change that because you are a collection of relationships between 40 trillion cells; between heart, lungs and brain; between muscles and bones; between thoughts, feelings and bodily expressions.

Life is not about things. Everything in life happens in relationships between things, operates in that in-between place of connection and interaction. It takes place in the axles. That is the nature, the essence of Relational Being. That is why wheels are no use in themselves. They need axles. Likewise, you need relationality. Without it, there's no life.

The in-between place is a part of the Field.

The Field is Real

How do you feel about this heading? The question is essential at this point in our journey. Broadly I see three possibilities: the first being that you still think this is all nonsense, in which case I congratulate you for still reading but warn you that it may not get any better. That isn't a point of view that can be changed by further explanation, much as I would wish it.

The second possibility is that you accept it, but it feels abstract and theoretical. It is less real than your usual thing-oriented perspective. That is understandable because so much of what I say goes against education, social norms, scientific "authority" and years of habit. I understand that feeling because it remains the same for me too, despite decades of investigation. Fortunately that is OK, provided you are willing to act as if it is equally real and make your choices and take your actions from that place. My experience is that we can fake it until we make it.

The third possibility is that you are completely on board and this is where you live your life. Good for you! As I see it, there are still many possible ways to navigate the space between the old and the new reality. Maybe what I will go on to say will help you with that or at least raise some interesting questions to play with.

Throughout this chapter I have been teasing out the creative edges of the Field, the Relational space and your position in it. I have done this in order to lead the way from Being to Becoming so that we can get the best out of shaping our world, individually and collectively. I have pointed to the way in which Law of Attraction etc. has failed to deliver.

Our focus in the next chapter is on our ability to listen and hear, because when you are dancing in the Relational Field, that is the music that you move to. It has rhythms, melodies and flows. If you can't hear them, or choose to impose your own inner beat regardless, the result will be graceless and unconnected. There is a form of Divine law that affects who we can be because it is maintaining the balance of creation across space, time and life. The music doesn't stop and will continue whether we are listening or not. We are more potent than we have known ourselves to be, but not omnipotent. It is a big Field of Possibility where you and I are dancing together with all that is NOT-YOU and NOT-I. How do we get the best out of that? What else is possible?

What could you know?

How are you getting on? Are you keeping pace with my repeated invitations to turn the map upside down or view the world from the inside out?

Is this multi-layered reality with its various layers of physical, mental and energetic aspects to your existence finding any place of recognition or comfort with you? You may have been on board from the start and finding it all to be plain sailing. If so, that is great, but I can't assume that. I know from many personal conversations that even people who are connecting in a spiritual way or who have had experiences that already created doubts about the conventional mechanistic and material worldview, do not find it easy to step all the way into an informational and relational existence. Believe me, I sympathise.

It is one thing for what I am presenting to make sense while I am explaining it. It is something else to shift your way of thinking to where it is natural to you. It has taken me quite a while. Fortunately, the good news is that you don't have to reach that point to begin receiving the benefits. I am saying all this now because we are about to take another step into what may not be familiar to you. I would like to help you over the threshold.

The title of this chapter is a shortened version of the question that drives what follows. What could you know, if all your sensing systems were awakened and you were able to receive the data that they provide? And that comes with some others. What could you know, if your perceptions were no longer filtered through old mindsets and preconditioned expectations? What might you be aware of if you were attuned to the flow of information around and through you? And if you were aware, what would that do to your ability to make the right choices, to connect with the people you need, to be in the right place at the right time?

"If only we could open our inner eyes", I said earlier. I asked, "What that would take?" That is what I would like to explore next, and I see two kinds of answer showing up right away. The first concerns how - the mechanics and techniques of connection, reception and interpretation. What does it take in practical terms to know all that we can know and locate ourselves in the flow?

Then there is the context in which that sensing takes place and the personal space that you create to live in that reality. I have been presenting aspects of that context all along, and much of it should feel familiar by now. At the same time this chapter is about making that more real, turning it from a concept into an application, from a philosophical perspective into a lived existence. We need to repeat and revisit, like turning a corkscrew into a wine bottle. It may seem as if we are going around in circles, but each time we penetrate deeper. That's the idea, at least.

Explaining Intuition

To begin the investigation of the mechanics of connection, which I will mainly call "Intuition" it would be helpful to get beneath the surface of that word, in both its meaning and what it is.

There are other words in use that pertain to our sensing of the non-material realm. We might sometimes say psychic, or call it ESP (extra-sensory perception) or sixth sense, or gut-feel. There are terms like clairvoyance (seeing pictures) and clairaudience (hearing voices). There are so many flavours of connection in this non-ordinary reality that we might easily get distracted from the big picture by stories of people who predict the future, or sense what their plants need, or stepping away from human experience, the dogs who know when their owners are coming home.

For our purposes, I wish to treat all these options as real and not to try to make distinctions, because the bottom line in my view is that all are different aspects of what is possible in a field of connected information. Since the information is everywhere, the only differences are in where and how people are engaging their attention and intention. So I choose to use the word intuition to cover all such phenomena. Everything that I am saying is about the way that we can connect to the contents of the field and how it can be used in all those ways and more.

Even though we have expressions like "gut feel" or "I know it in my heart" it is quite likely that you will tend to regard intuition as something that you do with your brain. If you search for images, at least half of them will come up with lights in and around the head. My experience is that it is helpful to park those perceptions because every part of you is connected, so every part of you is capable of receiving from and resonating with the Field. Indeed, since the Field is always present, you are doing so the entire time.

To explain how intuition works, I will talk about how I had my perceptions opened in the lead-up to that first intuitive experience. It occurred at the end of a 4-day training in "The Silva Method" (aka Silva Mind Control), a course developed by Jose Silva many decades ago. This is not the only way, and many other developmental approaches are available, but his method was very systematic and illustrates some key features that I believe are generalisable and have incorporated into my own trainings.

1) Get your conscious mind out of the way. Some people do this with drumming, trance-dancing or psychedelics[26], but the course uses a combination of deep relaxation and guided visualisation. Jose was also decades ahead of the recent interest in harmonising left- and right-brain modes of function and used sound to support the regulation of brain-waves to achieve a predominance of Alpha rhythms (8-11 Hertz) and reduce the usual waking state Beta waves (12 and above).

2) Refocus your awareness towards your inner sensing. Reduce the focus on your sight and hearing. There is a

[26] I regard these as useful tools for opening your system to new and different awareness. The downsides are firstly that they alter the process of awareness itself and may introduce their own influences into the field and secondly that they create a requirement for special conditions rather than supplying you with a new set of capacities for everyday life.

combination of intention and attention at play here. There are many forms of mindfulness and meditation available and you may have learned one yourself. They may involve emptying the mind, or shifting awareness into new habits and may or may not have elements of what I am about to describe. Jose Silva replaced the definition of ESP as Extrasensory Perception with his own "Effective Sensory Projection".[27] As a result, the awareness of inner sensing referred to is at the same time projected outwards towards the thing being sensed. This was what enabled me to detect David's brain tumour, by projecting my awareness into his local portion of the Field.

3) Include your awareness of what the body is detecting. Your heart's energy field extends a few metres beyond your body and sends more information to the brain than it receives from it. There is wisdom in our use of phrases like "gut-feel" and "I feel it in my bones". If you have experienced kinesiology, you will have seen that your muscles can "know". Many meditation techniques begin with the relaxation of muscles to become aware of what is present, and all approaches follow the yoga tradition of using the breath as a means of regulating bodily systems by creating heart coherence and calming activity in the vagus nerve[28]. By focusing on the body, we simultaneously reduce background noise and increase our ability to detect the signals that matter.

4) Learn how your system works. It became clear to me in teaching that it is as true in this realm as in others that we don't all work the same way. Far from it. My system works kinaesthetically – I feel something first and the words come later. Occasionally I would get answers as snatches of songs. I had one journalist student who "saw" the answers

[27] Or sometimes as Extended Sensory Projection
[28] See Alan Watkins' TED talk for a powerful demonstration of a centering process of this kind.

to questions as if scrolling up on his computer screen. Others hear the words, and some get pictures and images.

5) Intuition may come through with clarity, but often it can be quite vague and fuzzy. It is often symbolic and dreamlike, with a language of its own. This calls for us to learn our own inner language so that we can decode what we get, and often requires practice.

6) The problem I see this generating most strongly and frequently for learners is one of trust. We doubt ourselves and have been trained as sceptics. The pathways that our brain uses to deliver information are initially indistinguishable from those we use for fantasy and imagination, which creates a sensation that we are "making it up". Practice and experience will get you past that. Over time, you can learn to detect the qualitative difference underneath.

Dancing in the Field

The way that I have described intuition, including my first experience, might lead to a perception that it is about answering specific and individual questions. Of course, it can be that. I might ask my body what it would benefit most from when looking at a restaurant menu. You might use it in place of your conscious thinking when choosing whether to swipe left or right on a dating app.

Maybe you have seen or heard of the film "Men who stare at goats". This has its origin in experiments conducted by both the US and Russian military to utilize remote viewing techniques for locating military installations[29]. Intuitive capacities can be practiced, developed and used in a near-unlimited number of ways. The healing intentions behind Jose Silva's courses are mirrored in a multitude of techniques. I don't want to discourage anyone from

---

[29] Targ and Puthoff: Mind-Reach

exploring those. At the same time, my focus with this book is different.

What might it be like to live as if fully connected to the Field? I say, "as if", but perhaps I should offer a better alternative – what might it be like to live fully from your connectedness? Can you imagine that? Connectedness is real and you will by now have gathered that our challenge is not to make connection but to recognise, acknowledge and embrace that way of Being. To inhabit it and to Be it. That is what I aspire to.

I said at the close of the previous chapter that the Relational Field supplies the music that we dance to. Earlier I quoted Buckminster Fuller's statement that "You cannot get out of Universe. Universe is not a system. Universe is a scenario". Scenario is the outline of a play, just as music is the rhythm of the dance. I urge you to grasp the full significance of these metaphors for our existence. The dance occurs in your relationship with the music. The play unfolds through a character's relationship with the outline, and how a situation may develop. In this instance the character is you. Your life takes place through your relationship to the broader realm of things, people and events in the world of "Not-I". At any point, there is a range of potential outcomes arising from the scenario and a range of possible movements with which you respond to the music. You choose from among those possibilities according to your desire for the outcome that you believe your choice will lead to.

It takes three to tango

We cannot control what happens, so when I describe this as a dance I hope that you are hearing the sense of flow and interaction it offers, perhaps the improvisation and potential artistry too. It takes three to tango because there is you, your partner, and the music. There are many people who talk about our ability to "create our reality", but often that is a psychological statement about seeing and feeling what we choose to. Some use that phrase in a Law of Attraction sense, so they are oriented towards drawing what they intend towards them. I am presenting something more substantial than that; describing it as a dance should not be seen as trivializing it. I want you to see something more fundamentally creative than that, a scenario where we are causing shifts to the flow of the Field and making things happen as a result.

I previously said of dancing in the Relational Field, "It has rhythms, melodies, and flows. If you can't hear them, or choose to impose your own inner beat regardless, the result will be graceless and unconnected." That limits what you can make happen, so your intuition is key. It is the gateway because any reference I have made to choices is contingent on awareness. Awareness and choice are the essence of this dance. Relational Being takes place in the presence of all that is NOT-YOU and your awareness of what is flowing in that space.

In that same paragraph I also said "There is a form of Divine law that affects who we can be because it is maintaining the balance of creation across space, time and life." That is a big statement. Huge. You may find it helpful to read it a few times before we move on to unpack it. What does it mean? Why would it be such a big deal?

The significance of Divine Law

This has nothing to do with Moses or tablets of stone. I am not referring to human laws but rather to how the universe operates. If you don't want to connect that with any form of God, that's OK because you can think of this as the laws of the universe and of creation itself. You can think of it as the inherent nature of the Information Field. I am also describing the fundamentals of sustainable dynamic systems.

To be sustainable, a system must be capable of maintaining internal balance because if it doesn't, it unravels and collapses. If you push a pendulum, it swings back. It can't simply stop, nor can it carry on swinging beyond its defined boundaries. It has its own simple mechanical laws. So -

o   Think of the Universe as being like a billion pendulums. To every action there is a reaction.

- o Then think of it like karma – what goes around comes around.
- o Think of it like energy which cannot be created or destroyed, only change from one form to another.
- o Think of it as a trillion relationships between the elements of creation, all taking place through the Field of the information that describes them and governs their interaction.
- o Think of it as an infinitude of quantum entanglements in which particles are connected through the information that they hold about each other.

That may all seem quite abstract. Maybe it doesn't seem to be about you and me. But it is. It's impersonal in one sense because it is not concerned about you as a personality or as a set of motivations. But it is concerned about you as a set of choices, actions and influences on the Field, because you too are an assemblage of information and you too are a component of the flow. As a result, the universe has an imperative to maintain its balance in relation to you. It may be doing that in amongst a million other balances that affect the field around you, but you are always in that scenario, and there is no exit. An imbalance may correct itself immediately or over lifetimes, but balance must be maintained.

It is also about you and me because the balances in the Information Field operate within the field of human consciousness as well as in other systems such as physical laws and those that affect living systems as a whole, such as ecologies. Life, as said previously, runs counter to the principles of entropy. That is true of life as a process and as an overall system because life builds up patterns of information. Entropy suggests that all the heat energy of the universe must eventually dissipate and reach a state where every part of it is at the same temperature. But something different is happening within those boundaries, and within the field of living systems are the informational principles that govern humans.

In our opening chapters we encountered the way that information within family systems may propagate across generations, for example in the way that constellations show patterns from your grandparents affecting your children. The Information Field ripples through time and space. Thus, balances must be maintained at that level or in that realm too, and your informational system is a part of that. Divine balance applies to you.

Can you handle the truth?

Many decades ago I was on a Reiki training and my system was in a very open state. In one session we were encouraged to ask a question and see what our intuition delivered.

I was at the beginning of a relationship that seemed a bit difficult, and I asked about that. I got very strong guidance – almost like a vision - which was unusual for me. It amounted to "DON'T". But I did, because it was what I wanted. The result was two years of struggle and grief.

I could give other examples where life (the Universe) was giving me signals that I was going against the flow, where I had made a decision and I wasn't going back on it. It took me a long time to learn that persistence and courage are good qualities, but not in the absence of awareness.

Behind such events is a more profound truth. When you are trying to enter the realm of flow, it is dangerous to cherry-pick. It doesn't work to only pay attention to the information that you like. Plus, intuition will not even begin to work if you have set preconditions about what you are willing to hear.

If you are hearing me tell you that you must give up free will and that you are no longer an agent in your own life, please step back from that. But what aspect of you is hearing the message in that way? Is it your small, limited, disconnected egoic self? Or is it your higher self, your soul knowing?

There is a price of entry to the world of flow where you function in harmony with the dynamics of the world. The price is the recognition that it isn't all about you and what you want, and that there may be some discomfort as we adjust to that. In our good moments, we want peace in the world and nourishing relationships with those around us. In our not-so-good moments we may be judgemental, or hold grudges, or seek recompense for the harm that we feel others have done to us. But you are not the centre of creation, and the universe is not responsible for the comfort of your feelings.

This is not a matter of whether you "deserved" something unpleasant or whether someone else received benefits that you feel they didn't "deserve". If you see God/Universe as some external judge who should align with your view of what is fair and just, you will only create trouble.

- o You don't know what other balances the universe is maintaining.
- o You don't know what your soul has asked for along the way that is now being delivered.
- o You don't know what karma is unfolding either for you or for others.
- o You don't know what aspects of Divine Law are in play
- o You cannot see the whole picture, which may be unfolding outside the boundaries of your time horizon.

If you want peace, then you must create it from within and through your actions. If you want a more loving world then it is up to you to <u>BE</u> that.

As a result, the truth that is available to you when you live in the Relational Field is not human truth, and even less is it your truth or my truth. It is what IS. The expression "Oh Lord, let thy will be done, not my will" is not to hand over all agency or to make yourself totally insignificant. You are still entitled to make choices. You can still be a co-creator of the world to come, but your input is made within the relational space; there you are a contribution to something much larger, with a broader perspective than you can ever have. The expression is one of surrender and trust in the unfolding of shared benefit. The music continues whether you are listening or not. We are potent but not omnipotent.

We will develop these themes further in the next chapter by exploring the varied intelligences that we bring to our engagement and the different aspects of being that our choices arise from. We are still engaging with the challenge of the upside-down map and the inside-out reality. It's a new way of seeing. Re-making ourselves in a new way for a new world still requires radical shifts in the way we think, and the way we interact with existence.

Different ways of seeing

"We are all able to know the world through language, logical-mathematical analysis, spatial representation, musical thinking, the use of the body to solve problems or to make things, an understanding of other individuals, and an understanding of ourselves."

Howard Gardner, Frames of Mind: The Theory of Multiple Intelligences, 1983

Just how far are you willing to go in peeling away the limitations on how you see the world? How much does the material reality we see mirror our expectations and preconceptions? How much less dense might it be, and how fluid are the dimensions of space and time?

In Chapter 3 of "The Science of Possibility", as well as bringing some evidence for intuition, I include some material from "An Experiment with Time", the 1927 book by aeronautical engineer J. W Dunne about his experiences with pre-cognitive dreaming. That is to say, he had dreams of events such as a rail disaster that would be headlined in the newspaper a few days later.

Even time is not what we think it is.

I ask those opening questions because the more time I have spent exploring these edges, the less predictable, less solid and more mysterious become the ways in which reality seems to present itself. And the question "how far are you willing to go" begins this chapter because I will present some of what I have experienced over the years, but I will also stand back from some of the edges that I have encountered more recently. Of course, you may have explored places that I know nothing of, but if some of what I describe is new, I wouldn't want that to create a new limit. And whatever you encounter, I encourage you to trust your own knowing and your own connection(s).

Multiple Intelligences

Every chapter in this book has brought a new way of looking at our world and our existence in it. Now feels like a good time to explore the different perspectives that we bring to our understandings, so I want to spend a short while talking about intelligences.

It has been over 40 years since Howard Gardner proposed that rather than the single IQ intelligence quotient, we should recognise that there are several. He listed eight, these being:-

- **Linguistic**: Our use of words and language

- **Logical-mathematical**: Our use of numbers and logic

- **Musical**: How we use music, sound and rhythm

- **Bodily-kinesthetic**: Our ability to use our body and physical movement

- **Spatial**: Manipulation of space and images

- **Interpersonal**: Our skill in recognising others' feelings

- **Intrapersonal**: Understanding our own feelings

- **Naturalist**: the natural environment

Since that time, Daniel Goleman has developed the theory of Emotional Intelligence (EQ) which expands the interpersonal and intrapersonal into a fuller platform regarding how we identify, understand, and use emotions positively to manage stress, communicate appropriately, empathize, overcome issues, and manage conflict. This began to address the problem recognised in Bell Laboratories, where it was apparent that some of the smartest people (think of Sheldon in "The Big Bang Theory") were not good at working with each other, and over time, its concepts have come to be central in team development trainings.

I will also add here, since it is especially relevant to this book's context, the concept of Spiritual Intelligence (SQ), which expands the relationships with others towards our relationship with the expanded context of higher self and deeper wisdom, and the way that we relate to a higher power or some sense of spiritual purpose.[30]

As you look at the list, where do you notice that an element is strong, or weak for you? Maybe you have the combination of bodily and spatial intelligence that makes you good at sports. Or you combine musical and kinaesthetic abilities as a dancer. Do you write and speak well? I would like you to notice that this is another element of our uniqueness, that we have a different mix of leanings and natural abilities and that this mix affects both what we become in the world and the way we look at the world. That might seem obvious, but don't take it for granted. Look for how much it has influenced you and shaped your life. Look at where you may have been pushed in directions that were not natural. That too might affect what you choose next.

I can see the way in which my natural leanings towards linguistic and musical intelligence contributed to my trajectory in life, and I can also see how I have developed other areas, sometimes intentionally and sometimes more randomly from how the world came towards me or what seemed to be necessary in order to function well. My low intrapersonal skills and my interpersonal skills too, were making a mess of my life and limiting my career development. I needed to change.

I draw attention to this because I want you to be aware that you are not stuck with whatever you start from. Development is possible. Emotional and Spiritual Intelligences are trainable and coachable, and assessment methods support those developments. You can take dancing lessons or learn a musical instrument. Maybe you won't ever be brilliant if it isn't natural to you, but you can be good enough to not always feel inhibited or left sitting out, and you can learn to hear more of what is happening in music.

---

[30] Cindy Wigglesworth's SQ21 offers a profound developmental journey through the key intelligences for leadership success because the qualities that make great leaders are emotional and spiritual.

Each of the intelligences can grow with attention and practice, and we have recently been exploring intuition. I believe that we have been learning here about something I will call "Relational Intelligence". That is not (yet) recognised, let alone subject to assessment methodologies. Still, it is what we are learning about as we dive deeper into how we respond to the world, and then how the world responds to us as the Informational Field shifts in the space between, altered alike by us and by other forces and influences.

Spiral Dynamics (reprise)

Since SD is a passion and a core expertise of mine, I don't want to unbalance this narrative in its favour by revisiting it here. At the same time, there is a reason why it is so important to me, so I don't want to underplay that. I encourage you to give full attention to the resources and explore SD more deeply than I will in the coming paragraphs. Even so, I regard the following reminder of what I presented as having a lot to offer by taking a different, more evolutionary angle of approach.

The core question that SD works with concerns not what you think, but WHY you think what you think. It asks what your priorities are in terms of what values you hold, existential values, not moral values. These values form a developmental sequence that applies at every scale of human activity, from individuals to human evolution. It is the same sequence as in the section on parenting, viewed now from the perspective of the human species.

The earliest humans lived a precarious existence where survival was key – how to feed ourselves, be protected from the environment and predators. This parallels the need for a human infant to be fed and clothed. Subsequently, as human numbers increased, we bonded in tribes, sought safety, created narratives of collective identity and continuity.

This pattern continues and the themes for the first six stages are briefly summarised in the table here, using the same colour code as before. I invite you to consider that we tend to see our existence through the lens of the stage that currently holds the most energy for us. Someone with Orange priorities will focus more on the money and the concrete outcomes, whereas someone in Green would be more oriented towards people and harmony.

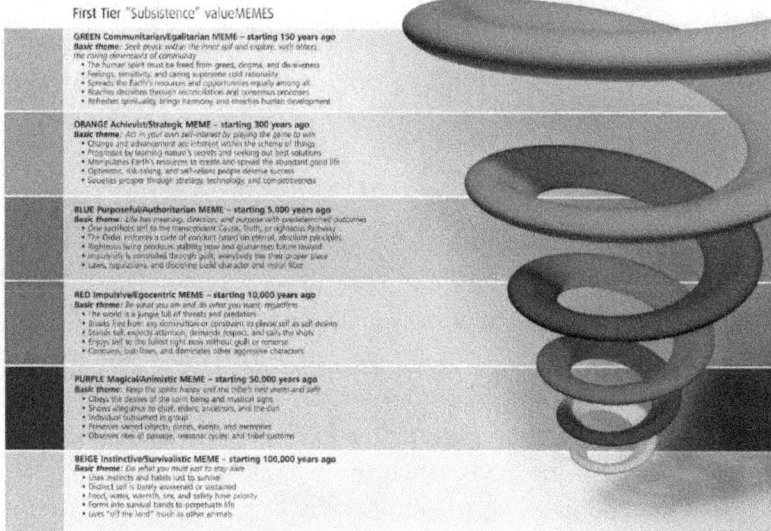

First Tier "Subsistence" valueMEMES

GREEN Communitarian/Egalitarian MEME – starting 150 years ago
Basic theme: Seek peace within the inner self and explore, with others, the caring dimensions of community.
  • The human spirit must be freed from greed, dogma, and divisiveness
  • Feelings, sensitivity, and caring supersede cold rationality
  • Spreads the Earth's resources and opportunities equally among all
  • Reaches decisions through reconciliation and consensus processes
  • Refreshes spirituality, brings harmony, and enriches human development

ORANGE Achievist/Strategic MEME – starting 300 years ago
Basic theme: Act in your own self-interest by playing the game to win
  • Change and advancement are inherent within the scheme of things
  • Progress by learning nature's secrets and seeking out best solutions
  • Manipulates Earth's resources to create and spread the abundant good life
  • Optimistic, risk-taking, and self-reliant people deserve success
  • Societies prosper through strategy, technology and competitiveness

BLUE Purposeful/Authoritarian MEME – starting 5,000 years ago
Basic theme: Life has meaning, direction, and purpose with predetermined outcomes
  • One sacrifices self to the transcendent Cause, Truth, or righteous Pathway
  • The Order enforces a code of conduct based on eternal, absolute principles
  • Righteous living produces stability now and guarantees future reward
  • Impulsivity is controlled through guilt; everybody has their proper place
  • Laws, regulations, and discipline build character and moral fiber

RED Impulsive/Egocentric MEME – starting 10,000 years ago
Basic theme: Be what you are and do what you want, regardless
  • The world is a jungle full of threats and predation
  • Breaks free from any domination or constraint to please self as self desires
  • Stands tall, expects attention, demands respect, and calls the shots
  • Enjoys self to the fullest right now without guilt or remorse
  • Conquers, out-foxes, and dominates other aggressive characters

PURPLE Magical/Animistic MEME – starting 50,000 years ago
Basic theme: Keep the spirits happy and the tribe's nest warm and safe
  • Obeys the desires of the spirit being and mystical signs
  • Shows allegiance to chief, elders, ancestors, and the clan
  • Individual subsumed in group
  • Preserves sacred objects, places, events, and memories
  • Observes rites of passage, seasonal cycles, and tribal customs

BEIGE Instinctive/Survivalistic MEME – starting 100,000 years ago
Basic theme: Do what you must just to stay alive
  • Uses instincts and habits just to survive
  • Distinct self is barely awakened or sustained
  • Food, water, warmth, sex, and safety have priority
  • Forms into survival bands to perpetuate life
  • Lives "off the land" much as other animals

31

The evolutionary narrative of Spiral development is that each stage was needed for us to adapt to the world we were creating. Purple, tribal thinking was sufficient for groups numbered in the hundreds. Cities need a larger perspective to hold their complexity, and as we have become more globally connected, we have needed the Green care for the whole to balance out the Orange competitiveness.

I previously referred to underlying laws of the universe which demand energetic balancing. The spiral is not as linear as I may have made it sound because all the stages remain present. Just because there are now many of us obviously doesn't mean that survival no longer matters. Nor does our need for core identity and belonging vanish; it remains an important piece of our psychological security. However, we have reached a point in

---

[31] Original graphics from What is Enlightenment magazine. Full article can be downloaded from the resources section of www.sdifoundation.com

development where the conditions we must adapt to are beyond what any of the first six stages can deliver on their own. We need them all, and we need them in healthy forms and in balance with each other.

That creates a need, one that much of humanity is experiencing. Something more is required. You will recognise the conditions we have created, ones where it is not only individual humans whose survival is at stake, but humanity's as a whole. We are overwhelmed by complexity, challenged by uncertainty and unsettled by volatility. We see the problems that we have created for the climate, for ecosystems, in political extremes and in migration patterns. That calls for a new level of adaptation, one that was foreseen by the original creator of the SD model and which he referred to as "the momentous leap".

I will focus on two aspects of this bigger change, where the first six stages, referred to as Tier 1, are succeeded by what will probably be a further six, of which two are present and recognisable. It is a shift from Subsistence to Being, and it begins with the process of integrating all tier 1 so that they are viewed as a functioning whole. That brings with it a systemic perspective where we are more capable of seeing all the parts of system as a dynamically functioning, self-balancing collective.

Second Tier "Being" valueMEMES

TURQUOISE Holistic MEME – starting 30 years ago
Basic theme: *Experience the wholeness of existence through mind and spirit*
• The world is a single, dynamic organism with its own collective mind
• Self is both distinct and a blended part of a larger, compassionate whole
• Everything connects to everything else in ecological alignments
• Energy and information permeate the Earth's total environment
• Holistic, intuitive thinking and cooperative actions are to be expected

YELLOW Integrative MEME – starting 50 years ago
Basic theme: *Live fully and responsibly as what you are and learn to become*
• Life is a kaleidoscope of natural hierarchies, systems, and forms
• The magnificence of existence is valued over material possessions
• Flexibility, spontaneity, and functionality have the highest priority
• Differences can be integrated into interdependent, natural flows
• Understands that chaos and change are natural

"What I am proposing is that the psychology of the mature human being is an unfolding, emergent, oscillating, spiraling process, marked by progressive subordination of older, lower-order behavior systems to newer, higher-order systems as man's existential problems change."
Dr. Clare Graves

Secondly, it involves a shift in our mindsets and ways of thinking, as our old ways are no longer sufficient to meet the new conditions. It requires us to let go of our linear narratives of cause and effect and to step away from our habits of polarised thinking, where we see alternatives that are right or wrong. Instead, we must see our choices as responsive to context and needing to be balanced. What was right a month ago may not be so valuable next month. We have to steer dynamically. Principles increasingly replace rules. This is the seventh stage and has the colour code of Yellow.

The eighth stage with its colour code of Turquoise, builds on the systemic perspective of the seventh. Where Yellow sees an overview of human systems, Turquoise adopts a holistic perspective of all life, encompassing our many connections to the planet, its living systems and its other inhabitants. There is an increasingly spiritual connectedness that resonates with the second, Purple stage, in which tribal groups connected through shamanistic experience to their land and to the spirits which animate their plants and animals. Thus, our earlier chapter with its stories of direct connection to the consciousness of horses illustrated a form of modern shamanism.

When taken in its totality, Spiral Dynamics is a meta-pattern of integration itself.

If you are so inclined, you can profile the pattern of your relationship to the stages in depth. The link is in the resources. For now, I invite you to look at the tables here and sense into the two strongest descriptions of your own priorities. Focus on how you actually are on a day-to-day basis as distinct from what you might aspire to become. You may also like to notice if there is one stage that you are most inclined to reject.

The point of this exercise is to recognise that we are exploring one more aspect of what makes you you. Where you are in the journey of your personal values and priorities is a significant factor in how you show up in the world, what influences your choices, and what shapes how you see the world and the others in it.

As you do so, please retain a strong awareness that what you see does <u>not</u> define you. The colour you favour is not a type because it can change. And while I have encouraged you to consider what is dominant, you are a mix of all of the stages. They are preference systems in you; they say what you value. And because the preferences are adaptive responses to the conditions of existence that are around you, they may tell you what your local field is shaping and, in so doing, may point to where external change is most desirable.

Spiral Dynamics is inherently relational. It is not hierarchical. It is also reflexive and recursive – creating mirrors between you and the world and looping back over the balances that are present in what we make important at any time. At this point in my life, I may be preferring the expression of my individuality (Beige, Red, Orange) over my wish to align with others (Purple, Blue, Green). In the former I seek to shape the world to fit me; in the latter I am more inclined to adapt myself to what society asks of me. There is no right or wrong about which you choose because they are balances in the living universe. Writ large, this is the dance of competition and collaboration that shapes ecosystems.

How we see the world

In a variety of ways, we are exploring the notion that we see the world not as it is, but as we are[32]. In framing this book around the question of what makes each of us the unique individual that we are, we are also exploring the way in which what we regard as real blends what <u>is</u>, with what we view it to be. Philosophers have debated this territory, and the question of what we do know or can know, for centuries. In my view, there has been no conclusion to that because no conclusion is possible.

---

[32] Variously attributed in modern times to Anais Nin and Stephen Covey, but with many echoes of earlier philosophies

That doesn't mean the question wasn't worth asking, but I suggest that it flags the need to take it lightly and to pay more attention to what we can usefully do with the knowledge we have.

Knowing what we know at this point, how, then, shall we live?

With that question we return to the central concern of this chapter and the one before, which is the way in which our non-ordinary senses engage with an underlying pattern of world-shaping information. How you apply your various intelligences is distinctive and particular to you. My experience as a teacher is that language-oriented people will find that their intuitive systems deliver their information as words, while visual intelligence people will see more images and those with kinaesthetic intelligence will also receive their perceptions accordingly, as feelings or whole ideas that are simply "known". More than that, what you get will be shaped around what is familiar to you in the exterior world. One person, an acupuncturist, when doing the psychic detection process, saw a mental image of the energy meridians lighting up. Allow your system to speak to you as is natural to it.

And as you do so, as you widen your perception of who you are and what the world is, continue to allow this shift from viewing reality as the material existence that we are accustomed to, to having the parallel awareness of a shaping field. You can live in both worlds, allowing the integration of left-brain and right-brain ways of relating to the world. Beyond that, stay open to the dynamic unfolding of that informing field, embracing that it is inherently emergent in its own flow and that it is also inherently shapeable, because, to whatever extent you are willing to allow, you are the field. You have no way of knowing where the boundary is between I and Not-I. You may not even see the boundary as significant. It is certainly not for me to say since I don't know anyway, repeatedly find my beliefs about the limits being cracked open, and I don't have the right to tell you how to BE. You are the flow and you are in the flow. It's your awareness and your choice.

What matters is the outcome, in your ability to create the life that you wish, the life that brings pleasure to you and contributes to the world in the way that you choose. The purpose of this book is to help facilitate that, to show as many aspects as I can of the layers of our human existence and expand the arena of possibility around what can be done with them. As we approach the end of this journey, we are changing the focus increasingly away from what has made you you, towards what will make the next you.

Who can you Be now? Who are you Becoming? What can you create?

Who can you be now?

"The future enters into us, in order to transform itself in us, long before it happens."

Rainer Maria Rilke, Letters to a Young Poet.

One answer to this question could be "anyone you want to be". That is true in theory, since the Information Field of You has no limitations. There is similarly no known limit to the power of the Divine to intervene in a transformational way. Miracles are possible.

Yet it isn't as simple as that, as we all know and experience. It is a paradoxical reality. Your day-to-day world is precisely that. It unfolds one day after another, in linear time. There is another world, one of precognitive dreams and influences on you today that reflect distant energies inhabiting your family Information Field.

There are stories of avatars, masters who can bi-locate their bodies. The Bible likewise has the stories of Jesus overcoming his own physical death and raising Lazarus. They are not in the linear, horizontal timeline but in another which is instantaneous, vertical, 100% in the present. Since I can't do that (yet), I can't speak to that reality. Thus what follows is mainly located in the linear frame. However, I wouldn't want to place any limitations on what can happen for you, and to a degree, what follows is about our capacity to bring ourselves 100% into present time.

What stops us?

There is a good chance you already know the general answer and have tried some of the many methods on offer. There are hundreds of them and thousands of books, videos and workshops, so I am not going to delve into details of methodologies. Instead, I want to talk about the principles, which I consider more important than any method. No method works well unless the engagement comes from the right place.

Wounds, Trauma and Safety

Life is not perfect. Things happen to us. Parents and families do not treat us exactly as we would wish. There have been impacts on our minds and bodies ranging from the minor to the highly abusive. We may be consciously aware of them or we may not, but awareness by itself does not produce change. In either case the effects are lodged in both body and mind aspects of the Informational Field. They may manifest as habits of thought and behaviour, as bodily tensions and stressed nervous system activity. In most cases, there will be a cluster of them such that it may take more than one technique or more than one type of support to release them all. As said before, this can take time.

We find it difficult to release any of these until we feel safe, so safety is a prerequisite. You need to be away from any threatening stimuli and then use techniques that support relaxation and letting go. There is a lot of information now about the role of the vagus nerve, and methods such as Havening, breathwork, gong baths and guided visualisations that will assist with general calming and nervous system regulation. This is the starting point for reintroducing coherence to your personal field.

As stated above, wounds and traumatic events such as abuse and injury, along with more subtle armouring against messages or responses that we perceived as threat, lodge themselves in our muscles and other structures. They also become embedded in our nervous systems and our patterns of thought. An example of a message that is perceived as threatening might be that you were regularly told that you were wrong, or bad, or a sinner. That might cause you to be guarded all the time against doing anything that might cause you to transgress, with the result that your system closes off any spontaneous impulse so that you can check for rightness. Knowing that someone in your family is easily triggered into anger could generate a pre-emptive response to that perceived threat. That might make you unnaturally quiet or submissive.

In these types of situations, your responses are events in the Information Field, equally likely to embed themselves in mind, structure or nervous system. It is possible that a technique which works on any of those could change the field in such a way as to release the others, but it isn't necessarily the case. Often it is like peeling the layers of an onion; getting to the centre can take patience. Meanwhile, the marketplace, whether through enthusiasm or manipulation, tries to sell you one-hit wonders and magic bullets. Of course, that is very tempting – who wouldn't want one of those? It is not my experience though, and it is rare among the many people I know who are engaged in this kind of development. For it to work means finding the right bullet for the right condition at the right time. The good news is that it is continually improving, as the field itself evolves with more of us engaging.

Lack of understanding

By now you will have grasped the message that humans are complex creatures. The various layers of our inner existence – spiritual, mental, and physical – combine with the multiple layers in the exterior – ancestral fields, cultures, locations, family patterns – overlaid or embedded in us through experience and education over time. That message impelled the writing of this book. Nobody tells you. At least, no-one told me, and all the messages I see out there are still oriented towards single facets of this brilliant-cut diamond.

Such limits to our understanding hold us back from experiencing miraculous changes and shifts by inhibiting the freedom for change to occur on all these dimensions simultaneously. We have only known how to alter the Information Field, one small piece at a time. I am not saying that I believe this is the only way it can be, and I think it can get easier. I don't want in any way to limit the realm of possibilities for you – just the opposite.

The challenge of mind-sets and programming

This may not be the last time that we revisit the central question of our mindsets. I repeat, what gets us into most trouble isn't what we don't know. Instead, it is what we think we know that is, in fact, mistaken. In saying that again, I am talking less about single facts than entire structures of meaning-making. I am referring again to the flawed and incomplete descriptions that come to us from conventional science. Even as someone who works with such ideas all the time I know from bitter experience that those ways of thinking are ingrained and persistent. It may well be easier for you if you know nothing about science, but you are unlikely to have totally escaped the cultural program for how the Universe works.

Accepting and engaging with the Information Field is essential to the shift. It is indispensable and crucial to the New Reality. Whatever you may have engaged with around law of attraction, creative visualisation, positive mindset or oneness will be amplified, multiplied in its effectiveness when no longer blocked by the restricted frameworks of outdated reality structures.

Science is not inherently bad. Left-brain information processing is a useful part of our way to engage with the world. Linear thinking has its value. Either-or choices may sometimes need to be made because we cannot both have our cake and eat it. Awareness of duality is inherent to your physiological existence and there would be little point in my writing a book for you to read if complete oneness was our daily experience.

I sometimes wonder if the loss of oneness is inherent to the differentiation that the Universe undertook from the moment of the Big Bang. It could even be the purpose of that event for all that is to experience itself through form. In any event, it appears to be the outcome. Although everything is ultimately connected in the field of information, you and I are parts, not the whole.

For the same reason, what you see is not reality and what I say here is not THE truth. At best it may sometimes contain A truth. By the same token, science provides us with what we can ascertain by breaking things down and examining their parts. Your cognitive brain processes what it perceives as facts, but these are not truths. Your linear thinking is time-bound, oriented to causes and effects, and single strands in the webs of interactivity. These limitations can be useful, but we also have to deal with paradox and the fundamental nature of both-and aspects of existence, of being at the same time wave and particle, living in a world that is both energetic and material. That requires us to step beyond those limitations.

I want to draw your attention to a less obvious feature of the psychic event that opened this door for me. In a few minutes, I was able to know something about David. That required no GP or hospital appointments, no blood tests or MRI. In an era which is filled daily with more data and with massive computing power to decode the information that is available, I want to highlight the contrast with intuition. The field will always contain more than any AI can. I invite you to embrace the conclusion that <u>information can be more efficiently ordered and accessed by intuition than by any other known means</u>.

Let's unpack that a little. I spend a lot of time thinking and much of the time I enjoy it. I find it interesting. Perhaps you can tell. I have also spent a lot of time thinking about things that I didn't get pleasure from. We all do. We all get stuck in figuring out what someone will do and what strategies we might adopt to prevent the undesirable behaviour. We think about a difficult conversation, what a boss or a partner might say, and what our response will be. At its worst, perhaps when situations threaten our well-being, we can spend hours in thought-loops of anxiety and depression.

Those situations are not typically filled with possibility, quite the opposite. We are in a loop because our usual thinking provides us with no way out. Logic and conventional structures keep us stuck. Our preconceptions about the world, our mindsets and belief structures trap us. What would it take for you to step away from all of that and open into something thoroughly new? What if you were to embrace the reality that everything is connected and that the field-aware part of you knows vastly more about the whole than your thinking mind ever can? You can't get your head around it, but you might let your head be inside it. After all, it is already there. You are already there.

What if you could let yourself go, drop into what was previously impossible? What if that is the space in which miracles can happen?

What will enable us?

The implication of already being there, already being fully connected, is that we need to embrace that fact. It is not new, but it is new to us. We need to live from that new reality. That is the source of who you are becoming.

Living from the new reality is essentially simple. It could even be easy. It calls for you to take a step into the directness of your relationship with the Information Field. Everything happens there. If you act in the material world, then whatever changes there is reflected in the Information Field. However, it can operate the other way around. A change in the Information Field affects the material world.

Every sparrow that falls

Earlier I quoted the gospel phrase, "Every sparrow that falls". The verse speaks to the idea that God is aware of and attentive to even the smallest details of life, irrespective of the degree of value that we give to it. It speaks of God's omniscience and is a metaphor for the completeness of the Information Field. It also holds the essence of the way that all of existence is held there.

The metaphor is also about God's care for creation and therefore, for us. The field cannot function without you. At the same time, please understand that I am not talking about the human sense of care. While the relationship is with you and in that sense individual, it is also impersonal, not sentimental or emotional. Emotions are for humans. The relationship is the outworking of God's law, which is a direct and true reflection of your existence, your Being in the field. The relationship is with all that you are and all that you have ever been, because that history is present in your karmic field:

- o   in what you have brought forward into your existence now
- o   in what persists in the field of your family constellation

- o   in the soul contracts that you made
- o   in the oaths and vows that you have made along the way and
- o   in the choices that you are making moment by moment, day by day.

That is a big list – maybe worth looking at again – to appreciate its full scale and dimensionality.

Does that sound as if it contradicts my earlier statement that living in this relationship with the field is essentially simple? After all, there is a great deal operating in all those layers of existence. But that is the nature of this book and the story I am telling. Even with all the layers we have explored, there is just you and the field; just you and God.

I am choosing to use that language at this point because we are accustomed to the idea of a greater power, omniscient and omnipresent. Blame Michelangelo. There's no question that we have contaminated that concept with our ideas of The Father, our images of an old white patriarch pointing his finger, with associated religious claptrap, and with expectations that God should care in a human fashion and should intervene in every situation from natural disasters to individual transgressions. Humans have projected onto God all that we would like God to be. We want Him[33] to be the power that we perceive ourselves to lack.

Many of us have residues of that projection because we grew up with it, just as you may have done with Father Christmas or the Tooth Fairy. I know this because I was raised as an atheist, despite which I imbibed that God with my school milk and compulsory morning assemblies. It is insidious, even though no harm is intended, because it fogs the nature of the Divine and the reality of our existence.

---

[33] My persistence with patriarchal terminology is deliberate, because it reflects what has been for thousands of years. This paragraph is about the way that humanity, en masse, has bought into that.

So, here is another thing to let go of, to put into the trash along with the limiting scientific constructs. Both inhibit us from finding the directness of our relationship with the flow of creation because both have the effect of creating priesthoods who seemingly will always know more about your existence than you can.

To hell with that.

Invoking a direct relationship

The relationship I have just described is as multilayered and multifaceted as the Field. That is not a problem though, you just need to meet your reality where it is.

At the most immense scale I have been describing the Divine in its totality, and you can speak to it at that level. While you cannot encompass the entire Universe, you can engage with everywhere that it meets you. That is enough. You can express your relationship directly without having to concern yourself with the precise nature of the contact points. Hello God, this is Jon. You can even think of it as a being. There is nothing wrong with talking to God as if it is an individual, and it doesn't matter if you think of that individual as male, female or an elephant just so long as you don't expect it to respond from human-like thinking.

And at the same time, each part of the Field has its own distinctness. There are no boundaries because everything is connected to everything else. Even so, you can engage with the sub-field that is your partner, your sibling or your manager. You can engage with your pet dog or the tree in your yard. Everything that is has its field of being. That includes elements of existence that do not at first appear to have a "life", yet the company that you work in is a living system and the town you live in is a living system. They have a history, a set of foundational beliefs, together with habits, cultural narratives, embedded contexts and characteristics that would continue to be theirs even if you took a job 1000 miles away.

They each have a life of their own, just as this book has a life of its own. It may have been my idea, though I am not certain of that, since it arrived in my thinking as something already part-formed at a time when I was convinced that I would not write another book. I was not looking for it. Far from it

That is not an anecdote. What the last two paragraphs have said is at the heart of the way you operate in the new reality. Since everything is an entity with its own existence in the field of information and its own unfolding there, everything is a Being[34]. Everything can be related to through the Field. This is the nature of Relational Being.

To make it easier and less abstract let me illustrate this in the human realm. If you have a life partner, there are three of you in the house. There's you, there's him/her and there is your relationship. This is not a foreign or novel concept, and I referred to it earlier when talking about axles. You might choose to "work on your relationship". Others might say "they have a great relationship". The arena where you meet is not in you and not in them, but in a place where you overlap. That overlap is in the Field.

I want to loosen the structure of that even more, because relationship is a noun, a thing-word. Just as Jon or ...(insert your name here) ... can appear to be thing-words. But you are not a thing. The Jon who is writing today is not the Jon who will be writing tomorrow, just as the Jon who existed in 2005 could not even have begun to write this. You too are a set of verbs, unfolding, changing and experiencing. You are the sum and outcome of that experiencing and it doesn't stop. You are a BEING, and being is equally a noun and a verb. Or neither.

Essentially, everything that makes up your life can be viewed as taking place in the Field, and you don't so much have a relationship as a relating. Relating is influenced from both directions. It is a mutual process, a dancing, a co-creating. It takes three to tango;

---

[34] As noted with the passage from Dorothy Maclean, that statement even extends to a pebble on the beach. Even though it is static, seems unable to change itself and may measure its change process in eons, it has a presence in the field.

you, the partner and the music. What you have is not a life but a living. That living is formed of multiple relatings, a thousand dances in a thousand areas of the Field.

This chapter title asks, "Who can you be now?" and we are dancing with the potential for miracles and for the Divine to intervene in a transformational way. We have looked at some of the potential blocks to our thinking and how they may arise from our experience, from our concepts of God and from our beliefs about the structure of the universe. And lastly we have been engaging with the open space beyond those blocks, the realm of possibility and the entry points into what will enable us to have our Being in that space. How does that look in practice? What do we have to do, who are you becoming and what will be the nature of your Be-ing?

Keep breathing.

Take your time.

And read on.

Who are you becoming?

"The real trouble with this world of ours is not that it is an unreasonable world, nor even that it is a reasonable one. The commonest kind of trouble is that it is nearly reasonable, but not quite. Life is not an illogicality; yet it is a trap for logicians. It looks just a little more mathematical and regular than it is."

G. K. Chesterton. Orthodoxy.

Before we get to the question above, a pause to ask, "How are you doing?" If you are reading these words, that is a good sign. You haven't given up. And as we are getting close to the finish line – at least for the book - I want to take a moment for reflection.

The previous chapter may have been a lot to take in. By its nature, this book is a lot to absorb, both because of how many aspects of your existence we have touched on and because of how many may have been new to you.

Most of all, this book presents a new reality, unfamiliar to most of us. My journey has spanned decades and is still a work in progress. If there is a finish line coming, it's really the start. I am reminded that American universities call their ceremony for graduating students a "commencement". Our closing chapters are your commencement address.

Create from who you are

I want to stay with the radical depth of what this new reality involves. Let's see what picture emerges. I can't tell you what to do, and you need to find your own way. It is the very essence of the process that you should do so; therefore, I can't give you a map. Instead, I can offer some insight into how you create your own map, and what it means for there to be more of us who are engaged with doing that.

The following sentence will surely fail to blow your mind. The future is unknown. Yes, you know that. But that doesn't stop millions of us from doing tarot readings, reading newspaper horoscopes or visiting psychics. Why do we do that? I suspect that it is because not knowing makes us uncomfortable.

That is not a superficial thing. At the core are some deep issues of existential fear, our inability to trust and the consequent search for control. Emotionally these are the essence of our challenge. Creating your own map rests on shifting your relationship with that challenge. Control is a major inhibitor to creation. Control does not provide us with a place of love.

Let me unpack that a little. In the previous chapter we encountered two of the major blocks to relationship with the Divine. If we don't even believe that there is a non-material, spiritual, informational realm, we are on our own. If there is no God, God can't have our backs. We cannot put our trust in the flow of the universe if we believe it is totally random and not connected to us. Even though there are other people around us, they are as much a part of our problem as solutions to it. How do we know that we can trust them? Is it any surprise that there is a lot of alienation, depression, anxiety and mood medication? In the UK, 1 adult in 6 is in receipt of mental health treatment, two thirds of which is pharmacological.

On the other hand, if we believe in a non-material realm, but view God as a punitive parent hostile to our own empowerment, offering free will in theory but only on the condition that we exercise that as the priests and their books say we must, we are forever monitoring ourselves against getting it wrong. When God's love is not unconditional love, our love of others and our trust in them cannot be unconditional either. How's that working out for the world?

When we cannot trust the flow of the universe, we are pushed towards the place where we think our only other choice is to control it. When we can't trust people, when it is so easy for us to find experiential evidence that they are not to be trusted, we have to control them too. Unless – the extreme option - we can get right away from them.

Families so often teach us this – even good ones - because the place where there is most love is also where we encounter a lot of control. The boundary between care and control is a tricky one. The control may be benign and well-intentioned. For many years the family IS our universe, or at least feels like it, and it shapes our model. How then do you step from the place of controlling our existence towards a place of creative possibility and the potential for miracles? How does your interior distinguish between Universe's care and the family's? How then can you see love as the best source of safety and the antidote to existential fear, so as to shift from control into trust?

You can't do this from your cognitive brain. It isn't wired for that. We can't figure out enough of the world because there is too much data to process. And while we are doing all that figuring, we can't simply BE. While we are controlling, we can't simply BE. What's the alternative that I am proposing here?

Finding flow

I hope that you can accept that there is some kind of flow to the universe. We all know that the sun will rise again tomorrow and that in spring there will be daffodils, or your local equivalent. We expect people to fall in love and have new generations of children.

Even while the world seems to be in greater turmoil than ever, we expect some continuity in our lives, and maybe precisely because of that turmoil, it is harder than it has ever been to know what form that continuity will take for us. How do we know what to do, and what choices to make? If you can't control it, can't figure it out, have already decided that numbing yourself with alcohol or TV soaps isn't helpful, you might feel strongly and even urgently, the need for something else.

This is that something else.

At this point I will assume that the message about the Information Field is beginning to land with you. Maybe more than that. You may be ready to engage your concepts of spirituality or the Divine as representing the way that humans have typically described that field, although it is not necessary that you should do so. What I will say can work for atheists too, since I am saying that the Information Field is a fact, just as gravity is a fact. You don't have to believe in them. You don't have to believe in weather either to know that there are flows we can't see, but which meteorologists display every day on your TV.

On that basis, I am inviting you to enter into an engagement with the weather system of your own life and I want to help you know more about how to do that. The principle is simple; if you expect rain tomorrow, you might change your intended activity, or at least your clothing choices would be different.

Awareness

An obvious question follows. How do I know my celestial weather forecast? I have already pointed to the answer when I said in the previous chapters, "information can be more efficiently ordered and accessed by intuition than by any other known means". Intuition is the means of access.

Everyone is intuitive, whether they know it or not. It is a skill that you can develop[35] for sure, but you don't necessarily need it. It is likely that you already have intuitive sensing and promptings. The problem is that you have not been listening to them, or, when you hear them, you doubt them and override them with the mind that you think is rational. You are not alone in that - quite the opposite. I only know a few people for whom that has not frequently been the case, and even fewer for whom it didn't take effort to overcome it.

What I describe as intuition is direct access to the Information Field. It resembles what happened to me when I connected with David and his brain tumour though it is typically less dramatic. In fact, it is often quite subtle, making it easier to ignore or override. You may already be engaged in direct access via other practices. For example, some forms of prayer or worship have a context of receiving God's wisdom. You may have done guided visualisations.

---

[35] Intuition training details: www.jonfreeman.co.uk

Some forms of healing encourage and teach you to sense the client's body. Some forms of meditation are active and go beyond "emptiness".

There are other embodied practices that lead you into your own non-cognitive awareness without ever referring to anything like the Field. They may even be presented as something purely internal – access to "higher self" or inner wisdom. For example, you might have a question that you ask at night with the intention that the answer will emerge through your dreams and be with you when you wake up. There are so many things that you may have already experienced without relating them at all to the Field. If you are active in any of those ways, great, carry on. Maybe do more.

I should also mention again that not all non-cognitive awareness is related to the Information Field. Our right-brain functions are always engaged in pattern recognition regarding events in our local environment. We are naturally sensitive to those promptings, too, but likewise trained and encultured to treat them as inferior to "hard data" and cognition. My view is that the boundary between these kinds of sensing and our access to the broader field is quite fuzzy, so blurred that we may not know the difference. And why would you care which of them you are using? What matters is increasing your awareness.

On the basis that you are already more engaged in these kinds of activities than you might think, my prescription is simple. Practice. Firstly, do more of them and do them more often. Secondly, give more attention to noticing what is there. That's it. Rinse and repeat. That is what you would do with any other skill, like playing the piano or snooker. Practice. Build new habits.

I should say something more and I suggest, important about noticing what is there. It may be words. It may be pictures and images. It may be raw ideas – fully-formed concepts that come before language or image. Then notice too, what is attracting your attention in the outside world. Your mind is often drawn to what it needs to be aware of. There are thousands of stimuli going on all the time, all around you, and you are screening them out as not relevant. You have to do that in order not to be overloaded, and for some hypersensitive individuals (e.g., maybe on the autistic spectrum) that can be a challenge. But your inner mind knows what is relevant to it and to questions that you are asking or to things that you need to know. Practice being aware of what you are aware of. You may be surprised by how much shows up, and how quickly. Don't underestimate the power of your inner mind. Ask, and you shall receive.

Choice

Now that you know what the weather is likely to be, you can choose what to wear.

Having said that, I need to soften the image of what that means. Maybe think of layers. If you weren't sure about the temperature or knew that it might vary, you would probably have clothes that you can easily take on or off and combine appropriately. That is a familiar concept for those of us who live in unreliable climates.

Or think about riding a bicycle. You are never perfectly upright. As you move, your weight shifts and you are always out of balance, but you learned how to compensate by continually adjusting. It is a dynamic process. Your body provides you with feedback all the time and you respond to it.

Choices are not decisions. Decisions are more fixed. You may be on the bike because you decided to ride somewhere. Of course, you could change that, but it is less likely. In the context of this chapter, I encourage you to think of your choices as dynamic. When you make a choice, the field changes and something shifts. The Field is dynamic and potentially there is feedback from it about the nature of the shift. Potentially there is a new space for your choosing. The shift may even make a new choice available that wasn't before. Develop that additional flexibility.

I am not trying to flood your life with uncertainty. I am reminded of a cartoon movie with a villain called the chameleon, who was eventually eliminated by projecting a light show onto him until he imploded with the stress of changing his appearance 10 times a second. That is not the idea here at all. But most of us are trained that we must make a decision and stick to it. Changing your mind may bring disapproval from others because they see it as flaky or lacking in persistence or self-discipline. I grew up at a time when people were expected to make career choices at 20 that would last until age 65. The world is filled with motivational stories about people who achieved their goals through dogged determination in the face of obstacles and rejections.

Nevertheless, this chapter is about your becoming, which is an emergent process of ongoing change through a responsive dance with the Universe itself. It too is changing. We are exploring a polarity between what is fixed and what is flexible, between what seems certain and determined (like the sun rising tomorrow) and what may change (like Trump's tariff rates and their effects on your personal, organisational or local economy). The Field conditions in which you made your choice yesterday may no longer apply today. Since the world in general is more complex, unpredictable and volatile than it has ever been, you need to be willing to flow with it. I am talking about an attitude, not a process. Hold your choices lightly. Don't fix them in frames of right or wrong, which lead straight to self-criticism and blame.

Complexity and flows

There is quite a lot to get used to here. How rapidly are you willing to step out of your linear, analytical programming? How ready are you to change the habits of a lifetime in order to have a radically different life.

Most of us would like life to be simpler than it is. The message here is that it can indeed be simpler, but not in the way that we have previously thought. In fact, hardly through our thought at all.

To repeat, the world is more complex than it ever has been. Globally, every human system connects to every other. A change in the economy affects migration patterns. A change in the climate affects food economies and water availability. A change in government policy can impact all of them. I could go on, but trust you get the picture. We are dealing with large systems filled with linked subsystems. All these human systems are embedded in planet-wide ecological balances that affect every living creature. We cannot make the world simpler. We cannot make our thinking much better at analysing the complexity. AI might help, but not in all areas and often not at an individual level. When your infant is awake at 2 am with teething pain, AI won't give either of you a cuddle.

More to the point, this book has been about the multiple layers of existence that have influenced and may continue to influence you. Thus far, no AI would know what is in your family constellation or what conclusions you drew from your birth experience. If you made a soul contract, I am working here on the assumption that it will never, ever have access to that. I am impressed by what AI can do and am certain it will do more. In theory, since everything exists in the Information Field, it is theoretically possible that an AI could directly and consciously engage there. Could you have a personal AI Daemon that does all that on your behalf? Maybe. But not for now.

So, how many flows are there? And since the answer is more than you or I can count or engage with analytically, we're again drawn back to the essential position that intuitive awareness holds for us. It is our only way to manage the complexity. It is your only way of stepping into the flow.

Letting Go

Listening to the flow, choosing and stepping into this new process of becoming calls for a lot of letting go. Mark Twain's observation bears regular repetition "It ain't what you don't know that gets you into trouble, it's what you know for sure that just ain't so." How much of what you have thought you knew or become functionally habituated to are you willing to let go of? Until that willingness is present, you are pushing water up the hill of your own hesitancy and reluctance.

Our mindsets and the habits that we have built around them are there because they have given us a feeling of safety. That is natural, human, and nothing to be ashamed of. At their root though, is an illusion. The safety is rarely real, and almost always unexamined. One illusion is that we know what we need, as in the well-known story of the zen farmer[36]. Another illusion is that those mindsets

---

[36] *There once was an old Zen farmer. Every day, the farmer used his horse to help work his fields and keep his farm healthy.*
But one day, the horse ran away. All the villagers came by and said, "We're so sorry to hear this. This is such bad luck."
But the farmer responded, ***"Bad luck. Good luck. Who knows?"***
The villagers were confused, but decided to ignore him. A few weeks went by and then one afternoon, while the farmer was working outside, he looked up and saw his horse running toward him. But the horse was not alone. The horse was returning to him with a whole herd of horses. So now the farmer had 10 horses to help work his fields.
All the villagers came by to congratulate the farmer and said, "Wow! This is such good luck!"
But the farmer responded, ***"Good luck. Bad luck. Who knows?***
A few weeks later, the farmer's son came over to visit and help his father work on the farm. While trying to tame one of the horses, the farmer's son fell and broke his leg.
The villagers came by to commiserate and said, "How awful. This is such bad luck."
Just as he did the first time, the farmer responded, ***"Bad luck. Good luck. Who knows?"***
A month later, the farmer's son was still recovering. He wasn't able to walk or do any manual labour to help his father around the farm.
A regiment of the army came marching through town conscripting every able-bodied young man to join them. When the regiment came to the farmer's house and saw the young boy's broken leg, they marched past and left him where he lay.
Of course, all the villagers came by and said, "Amazing! This is such good luck. You're so fortunate."
And you know the farmer's response by now...
"Bad luck. Good luck. Who knows?"

and habits have given us control at all. As we saw earlier, control is what we seek when we don't trust. It helps us feel less vulnerable.

I recognise that in encouraging this transition from analytical to intuitive, from left-brain to right-brain, from material world to informational world, I may push you towards feeling "better the devil I know than the devil I don't". If your highest priority is to feel safe, that may be hard to overcome, so I want to highlight some other possible priorities. What really matters to you?

- How important is it for you to have deep bonds in your life with family and "tribe", either the ones you were born into or the ones you have adopted? The "analyse and control" route will not be ideal for that. It holds back the things that make them feel trusted, and you feel emotionally connected

- Where are you looking to feel personally empowered and able to express all of who you are in the world? Analysis and control increase the extent to which you will hold yourself back and comply with others' expectations in order not to be disapproved of

- Where would you like a greater sense of "doing the right thing", not in the sense of obeying the rules, but rather in operating by the correct principles and expression of moral values? In a world whose rules and practices are regularly leading away from that "rightness", analysis is likely to take you down its path, not yours

- How much do you desire to break through the limitations that you sense are holding your life back, impeding your success, and getting in the way of your goals? Safety is not a bad thing in itself, but if it is not put into a healthy balance with your entrepreneurialism, your sense of strategy and your intention to be the best you can be, then you will be too averse to risk. Your analysis and control will be paralysing.

- How important to you are a sense of harmony, of human awakening, of fairness and human bonding on a planetary scale? These are all decreased when you are disconnected from the flow and constrained in your ability to feel and sense the good of the whole.

If you have a sense that these are deeply transformational times, that shifts are happening at levels that we struggle to see, but which you know from somewhere deeper to be arising as a potential in the Universe, then you are aware that something is waiting to come to fruition. Engaging with the framework of the new reality and with your full relationships in the Information Field are the means by which you, and all of us who so choose, can be part of bringing that about. Being that and Becoming that are our journey and our destination. That is where we will go in our final chapter.

The Future: What Will Make Us WE?

"Thus though man has never before been so complacent about what he has or so confident of his ability to do whatever he sets his mind upon, it is at the same time true that he has never before accepted so low an estimate of what he is. That same scientific method which enabled him to create his wealth and to unleash the power he wields has, he believes, enabled biology and psychology to explain him away – or at least to explain away whatever used to seem unique or in any way mysterious. ... Truly he is, for all his wealth and power, poor in spirit.

Joseph Wood Kruth, literary critic and naturalist. Human Nature and the Human Condition.

So much more I could say, so little time.

Life is filled with paradoxes. Our logical minds may want a life without inherent contradictions, but life doesn't. Creation happens in the dance between seeming opposites. Earlier, scientists sought to understand all the rules because they believed this knowledge would reveal the mind of God, and everything would become predictable. God-mind is not human-mind. Evolution and emergence happen in the space of illogic. Paradox creates possibility.

The science underpinning this book is as real and well-founded as it gets, but it is not certain. It is good enough to work with, and better than what most of us have had until now. This book is a small snapshot and overview rooted in both science and experience – not just my experience, but a mass of reported human experience. Neither scientific investigation nor human experience stops – quite the reverse, since there are more humans alive and experiencing, with more of them doing science than ever before.

While there is enough here to be going on with, I want to touch on a couple of other aspects that you will come across so that they can have a functional place within your worldview and your sense of what to do next. I will start with frequency because so many people talk about frequency and about raising your vibration. Let me build an image around that idea.

I haven't described how information in the field is encoded. I hardly know and I don't think we need to. You don't need to be an engineer to drive a car. I do know that a homeopathic remedy can be made using a vibrational frequency as an alternative to working with substances, and that other healing modalities work through resonance between energies that are in the frequencies of colour, or crystalline matrices. Bio-tuning uses sound frequencies to deliver its changes to your body. I could offer many more such examples. My working hypothesis for now is that the Information Field is encoded in frequencies – vibrational combinations of them. Since there are millions of frequencies, and they can operate in millions of combinations, this would result in nearly infinite numbers of codes. Since they may also interact in complex and dynamic fractal patterns, the encoding may be very far beyond our analysis. It is probably just as well that we don't need to know and instead focus on our coherence and clarity.

While stating that we don't need to know, I also want to mention briefly that I am fascinated and often amazed by the constantly emerging information. In the resources section, I include references to the work of Veda Austin and Robert E. Grant on how frequencies are encoded within the various structures water can take, and how the information I mentioned under the headings of constellations, ancestral patterns, and your genetics might be present in the water of your cells or the amniotic fluid in which you developed. Water connects all living systems, so it's not surprising that the Information Field influences that as well, creating an intermediary between the information itself and cellular function. That may be a component of what the following paragraph describes.

Your body contains trillions of cells. Using that image, each of them would have its own combination of elements – descriptive frequencies in the Field that forms it. Each cell is a life form with a cell wall, a nucleus and other chemical structures based on what a single-celled life-form needs for its existence. You can think of yourself in that sense as a metropolis of cohabiting cells. Each of those was created by the information in its DNA – your unique DNA, as detective stories will tell you. Thus, your unique DNA has its own distinct Information Field within the matrix of creation.[37]

You also understand that you are more than just a solid physical object. Since everything is encoded in frequency, you can see yourself as vibrating radiance or a light body. Whatever appears in aura photographs is one expression of you. Any aspect that exists beyond your physical form—such as your soul or spirit—is also a collection of frequencies stored in the Field's memory.

Form is the shape of Consciousness

This infinitude of frequencies is what makes the universe. If I were to make a cross-stitch sampler to put on my wall in the style of the 19th century, it would say, "Form is the shape of consciousness."[38] If you can get fully inside this concept, you will know all that you need to know about the New Reality. It is essential to note that "form" here includes forms of behaviour, thought and context. We haven't begun to understand how that works because that requires not only knowing how information is encoded, but how its patterns operate over time. Of course, I may turn out to be mistaken about the mechanisms, but I am close to certain about the nature of the relationship.

Consciousness has so many different meanings that I need to be as exact as I can about how I am using it here. I am appropriating it to denote the biggest possible picture, all that the Universe knows about itself, the Information Field, the Mind of God, the Star Wars

---

[37] If someone tells you that your DNA is the vibrational matrix through which all of connection operates, they may or may not be correct. Since I have been saying that our connection is a whole-body function, I don't think it matters. It is as good an image as any.

[38] Juliet and Jiva Carter www.thetemplate.org

"Force", the Source or whatever equivalent you might put there. And within that big picture are myriad subdivisions, components and sub-fields from sand-grains to moths to you. Your soul, your Atma, your spirit, your own individualised portion of consciousness exists there. Your form, your soul's form and your physical form are all equally the shape of your consciousness. In effect, where others refer to consciousness I would posit the presence of a Field of Information, or a collective of them.

I have been repeating an invitation for you to look at the world and your place in it from that perspective, to engage with your existence as a vibrational matrix, and to make your local Information Field your primary focus. Since form is the shape of consciousness, your vibrational matrix runs ahead of your physical existence as the generator of who you can be. It is the source of your existence in the world, the locus of your being and your becoming, and the source of your creation. It is the place from which you relate to everything that is not-you. With apologies to Rumi, between you and I is a Field. I meet you there. That is where relating happens. Where relating happens is where our cocreation takes place.

I invite you to pause, consider and even re-read and contemplate the last three paragraphs. They are offered not as theory but as a transformational statement about how you might see yourself. I encourage you to take them in at the deepest possible level.

Language, Truth and Logic[39]

This material is challenging to write and may be tricky to read because the language we have is the way we have encoded the meanings that we have previously made of our world. Forgive me for the writing and forgive yourself for any part of the reading that feels like a struggle. We are rewiring our brains in order to make new meanings. When I use the phrase "new reality", those new meanings are what I am really talking about. Reality has not changed – the world is as it is and has always been. This is only new

---

[39] After A.J. Ayer and the first philosophy book I read.

for you and me. That means it has to be new IN you and me. It's an inside job.

We encountered the language challenge previously when I encouraged the fresh perspective that we are not nouns but verbs. Jon is not a writer, he is writing. Beyond that, I am not an experiencer and I am not having an experience. I am experiencing. I am the experiencing in action. I am not a human body having a Divine experience, nor a Divine body having a human experience. I AM the experience, human and Divine[40].

Please breathe that notion in and sense where you stand in relation to it. What would it mean to you to live from that space?

Language evolves slowly and it could take generations to change in ways needed to express the truth of this existence. Maybe as we operate more in the Field and in the intuitive experiencing we will have less need for language. Truth itself is a tricky concept because in a world of continuous becoming, what is true is not static and fixed. The Field is ceaselessly changing. And the more we function from the non-linear, non-cognitive and intuitional mind, the less we can operate from the historical forms of logic. Sorry, Spock, but that is why Capt. James T Kirk always insists on not being told the odds. Jim Kirk knows that the odds have something to do with him.

So, what of this language of "raising your frequency" and "higher vibration"? With apologies for mixing my sci-fi references, I want to quote Yoda,[41] "Luminous beings are we, not this crude matter." All movies with magic in them - Lord of the Rings and Harry Potter being

---

[40] Indigenous **languages**, like Anishinaabemowin, are 80% **verb**-based, which similarly highlights the importance of relationships, acting together, and the plurality of being in this world. In contrast, **noun**-based **languages**, like English, tend to emphasise categorisations, dualisms, and classifications.
Verbs Not Nouns: How language can shape alternate worldviews | Now Then Sheffield
Sapir-Whorf Hypothesis
[41] Star Wars, Episode V "The Empire Strike Back". Luke and Yoda on Dagobar.

similarly popular examples - express an underlying human belief in this other view of reality. I don't believe this is wishful thinking; we know instinctively that more is possible. We sense and feel the patterns within, the archetypes, the unseen forces. It may or may not be the case that the future we desire has higher frequencies than the ones we dwell in today. I certainly experience a sense of lightness in how my body feels when it is resonating with what will be good choices for it. But does it matter what the frequencies are? I suggest that concern over that can be a distraction, and sometimes an invitation to measurement, to comparisons that are not healthy, and to judgements. I prefer to treat them as metaphors.

How then, shall we Live?

The title of this chapter plays with meaning and paradox. Linguistically it makes marginal sense to say "What will make us, WE?". Whatever sense you might make of it is paradoxical. I see that paradox as a central element in our unfolding, our emergence, our commencement. I also see reason to think that this collectivising of our awareness is already happening; we are sensing one another and the shifting of the world alike from our soul consciousness. The boundaries of time and space are dissolving. Are you sensing that too?

Just as there has been a perennial challenge around oneness and the illusion of separation, there is another around self-development versus human emergence as a collective, just as there is a tension in the world in our relationship to non-human parts of creation. When a mosquito lands on my skin, I am not a Buddhist. I give my life-form precedence over its'.[42] That attitude, scaled to a planetary level, is a feature of our existence. We have thought ourselves more important. To date, that seems to be the same as any other species.[43]

---

[42] I generally avoid killing creatures that are not attacking me. There are more spiders in my house than some people would tolerate.
[43] The compelling evidence from Jane Goodall's studies of chimpanzees is that under certain conditions primates will also kill members of our own

You will make your own choice in this area. Indeed, I am insistent that you must, and that neither I nor anyone else should tell you what to do. However, I think it matters what frame we have around our choosing. I have suggested the value of meeting the field of the universe, establishing a relationship with it, and becoming aware of the flow so that our choices are harmonised with the movements of the universe. That is a great leap forward. Even so, I will add to it, with the intention that we can co-create a future that meets the needs of all.

The question "What will make us, WE?" engages with the tension between individuals making their own best choices set against the needs of the human collective, or even the planet. Is this a distinction without a difference? Almost. We are all part of the same system, the same planet, in which interdependence means that there is no such thing as thriving on my own. Should I be able to trust that intuitive choosing will take care of that tension by itself? Again, almost. The flow takes care of a great deal and limits the extent to which I might choose something harmful.

Even so, we are part of the creative force, nudging the universe in the direction that we want for ourselves. I suggest that it could be even better if we have a shared sense of direction, one that intentionally includes other humans and the planet. How can we do that when we don't really know what others need or how the planet functions as a whole?

Once again, unsurprisingly, our analytical minds can't unpack that question. Our analytical minds, our left-brain functions, are oriented to a thing-based reality. They are not suited for choices beyond the level of what we might physically cause to happen, and where, and to whom or to what. Those ways of thinking tether us to that thing-oriented reality and to specific outcomes. It is the same error as has caused us in the past to believe we can intervene in

---

species. The roots of human violence and warfare are also found in our closest genetic relatives.

systems beyond our understanding, propelling us rapidly into the Land of Unforeseen Consequences. So what's the alternative?

Welcome to the land of Quality

Typically, when people present the science that describes our engagement with the energy reality, and wish to support our potential to operate differently, there is a stampede towards quantum theory. Understandably so, since until now it has been our only entry point into a realm that exists below the level of visible matter. The chances are that you have encountered explanations of the observer effect, the idea that what is undetermined in the quantum realm is influenced in one direction or another by our actions in looking at it and deciding which possibility we are witnessing. They are not wrong, but such explanations are insufficient.[44]

Humans don't think in quanta. It takes more than that. We need to meet the Universe from where we are. We need to meet it as Beings and from Being. In addition, believing that we are making choices about the state of matter (even when operating at the boundary where energy becomes matter) takes us again towards thing-oriented conceptions. It repeats the pull into an analytical way of engagement – unsurprisingly since that is the conceptual base for the underlying physics.

The alternative is for us to engage at the level of our senses, our feelings and our intentions. These are not quantitative in nature, but qualitative. Rather than talking about quanta, we need qualia, the perceived sensations and qualitative distinctions between one way of being and another. That is so much easier. It might sound more difficult, but that is only because it is an unfamiliar language. In fact, it eliminates a lot of decision-making and argument from the picture. In 2025, let's say we are examining what needs to happen in Ukraine. Our quantitative thinking brings all the arguments about

---

[44] I explain their inadequacy at greater length in "The Science of Possibility", chapters 13 and 18

defence policy, armaments, what to do with Putin, where to draw borders and how to negotiate a cease-fire. Qualitative thinking and engagement with the Field of Information instead places those details into its emergence. It's like saying "figuring this out is above my pay grade" and delegating the details upwards to a system that has more intelligence.

This is equally true at the individual level. There is a great deal of material in New Thought and New Age about how we create our reality. Much of it is based on "resonance", in "being the frequency of what we want to manifest" and similar expressions. It once again enters the realms of "raising your vibration" and broad assertions that positive thoughts have higher vibrations than negative ones. It is central to David R. Hawkins book "Power vs Force".

As with the quantum explanation I don't wish to say that these descriptions are wrong. Hawkins' book became popular and was renowned for good reasons. These approaches all head in the right direction, but because they lack the context of the Information Field, they are more difficult to work with. They draw our attention to measurement of our state, to concerns about our emotions, to a need to know what those emotions are, and often to a belief that our creative visualisation needs to be specific. What if the Universe could take care of more of that?

Here's a tangible example. I remember being taught many years ago that when trying to create a relationship I should be specific about blonde or brunette, age, body type etc. The more exact I could be, they said, the greater my chances of creating my perfect relationship. My experience is that it doesn't work; it's conceptually flawed and hard to do (what if you leave something out?) and gets you stuck in your head. It preferences control over trust. The 25-year marriage that followed that period would not have matched any list I could have written, and I am deeply grateful for it.

What if what you really need, what would nourish you and develop you, doesn't fit your preconceptions? What if you had a soul contract with someone outside the limits of your current knowledge or field of view? Instead, maybe it would be better for you to be asking the universe for a person who will love you, expand your life in wonderful ways, be fun to share your life with and take your journey in the direction that your soul is calling for. What if you stopped believing it is your job to control? What if you came to that interaction in a spirit of curiosity, asking where you might be led that is beyond your limits and in realms of possibility that you haven't considered?

Create your reality

There are two ways to interpret this heading. One is interior and concerns our perception of what is real, what we give meaning to and ascribe value to. It is mind over matter in the sense that if I don't mind, it doesn't matter. This book is not about that.

The second is exterior, the view that what is taking place in the outside world can be altered by how we interface with it. It has forms that vary along a continuum from passive to active. The first is about creating a resonance within ourselves that forms an attractor field for the unfolding fractal chaos of the Universe around us, and is often called "The Law of Attraction". The other polarity of the continuum is that by whatever means – quantum influence, observer effect, etc. – we actively alter the unfolding chaos. We are the butterfly wing beat that can eventually lead to a hurricane.

Somewhere in the background of these are older ideas that show up in religious sacrifice rituals and prayer. I am not going to enter a debate about "magical thinking" and whether that is primitive, childish, or a form of something real. I am only pointing out, as context, that people have always invoked outside forces in some frame of interaction and influence.

Relational Being operates in the realm of active influence. In the space where your Information Field meets the Fields of other entities and actors, and through that connects to the Information Field as a whole, there are possibilities for interactions that can generate change. Our choices can influence the direction of that change and the quality of existence that it leads to. Relational Being puts us in the position of co-creators. When we engage with that qualitatively, we open the portal to the existence we desire.

A qualitative invitation to the Universe opens up a wide and more flexible set of possibilities, in which we can hold and generate from a sense not only of what I want, but where that can sit in a context of all life, including other humans and the panoply of living systems. My creation is taken away from any tendency it might have to self-centredness, egotism or a narrowed focus. As a result, we invoke more of the Field, engendering a resonance with others who are doing likewise, and thereby we amplify our effectiveness.

The paradox of "my will"

I am strongly inclined to believe that our individual creation is more potent when our intention is strong. The butterfly can beat its wings more powerfully and more frequently. Our ability to manifest our intention is in some measure a product of our desire to make it happen, our belief that it is possible and our expectation that it will show up. This was a key element in what Jose Silva taught, and his training marked the beginning of my journey.

This may sit strangely against what I said in the previous paragraph about self-centredness and egotism. It may seem like a paradox. Yet, this tension operates dynamically at the heart of Relational Being. Jose Silva was equally strong in repeating the phrase "if this is for the benefit of mankind". Thus the tension is central to Relational Being because nothing takes place in isolation. Instead, everything takes place in relationship to the Field as a whole. Specifically, it mostly occurs in relation to the aspects of the field that are most local to us, including the people, other life forms, organisations, and other parts of the flow with which we interact most.

Creating resonance is both an inside and an outside job. In the physical realm we can act against others, and people do so. In the spiritual/energetic/informational realm this is much harder to do. Resonance depends on coherence. The old radios were filled with crackle and hiss because of how much was interfering with the signal. If that isn't part of your own memories, you have seen it in movies where the message, or lack of it, can be crucial to the plot. Similarly, if your signal is not clear, the Universe will find it harder to hear you. If you put out internally contradictory signals it doesn't know what to respond to and cannot mobilise change in the Field. If you put out signals that conflict with the flow of other signals around you, the Universe is operating with those external contradictions which cancel each other out. Universe is thereby inhibited from responding to signals that would cause harm to others, whether intended or not.

As a result, our co-creation with the Universe cannot be forced. Willpower is ineffective in the Field when congruence is absent. Dealing with incongruence requires inner work, taking care of "shadow" and dealing with whatever other influences have become part of your Being. Whether you do so and how you do it is also a choice. I am not saying that anyone is wrong or bad for not doing so; I am merely asking you to recognise it and suggesting that the choice is becoming more distinct. It is the price of entry for what follows.

You may be aware of a strong and powerful current of transformation. As mentioned earlier, this is a very widespread perception that views the coming years as a time of significant shifts occurring at a level that may not have happened for millennia. I am inclined to believe this and to hope that this book contributes to it. Many presentations of this transition characterise it in ways that are beyond what we have previously considered possible. Since I don't know how this might turn out – indeed, since I view the results as potentials in the flow and not pre-determined – I believe that the outcomes depend on what we do with these flows of energy. Similarly, that not-knowing also says that the possibilities are not limited. How big are you willing to let your vision and intention be? Are you willing to have it be limitless and play in the space of full personal and collective potential?

Create from who you are. The paradox of the new I

The co-creation I have just described morphs a blend of our personal empowerment and influence into a shift that occurs at the level of our species. Robert E. Grant encapsulates this paradox neatly with the term "omni-solipsism". In the African proverb, those who would go fast, go alone. If you want to go far, travel together.

In the spirit of invoking limitless thinking, I don't wish to constrain your intentions for personal fulfilment and success. Our heads are full of winner and loser imagery. That is the way the world has been – constructed from competition, scarcity and win-lose scenarios. Instead, the new I is also a We. We can create a win-win world for us both. More than that, there is the possibility of the third win that benefits you, me and the system/planet. How does it get any better than that? As described earlier, this is how evolution has operated, with organisms collaborating to build the next collective. Are you up for creating that?

This form of co-creation can also include your soul if you draw that into the frame. If you have any concept of a higher self in that way, why wouldn't you? Here too, you don't have to figure it out, you don't need your mind to know what your soul wants. You don't even have to decide whether you believe in a soul. Don't worry about it. Your soul would be an element of your Information Field, so the more you get your cognitive planning head out of the way, and the more you move from control into trust, the more space you make for it to speak directly into the field of creation.

The Ultimate Strategy and the Highest Vibration of All.

Blending individual empowerment and self-actualisation with the recognition that we are unavoidably all in this together is at the heart of the chapter's title question. If raising our vibration matters, it would mean stepping away from our emotionality. That would be a good thing to do for yourself, and it could only benefit those around you and the wider collective. Therefore, practice rising above all the noise and drama to see it from a higher perspective. Watch the dance – or even the riot - from the balcony. Emotions reduce your coherence, and you don't have to engage. Not your circus, not your monkeys. If there is something you can do to change a situation, by all means do it. Otherwise, may you be granted the acceptance to live with the things you cannot change. Surrender that to the universe. Give it to God. Other people will have to deal with their own development and their own karma.

If raising our vibration means stepping more into love and kindness, that would be the best thing, the most healing thing we can do for ourselves and our bodies. What reason would there be for not BEING that? It can only benefit you, and at the same time it will benefit those around you and the planetary whole. Practice making that step. If there is something that you can do to help others, do it. If not, bless those who can, and trust the Universe to unfold as it needs to. Use your intuition and awareness to find the right place for you in the unfolding.

Love and kindness are the ultimate personal strategies. Embrace all that you are and let everything else fall away. They are also the ultimate strategy for our planetary future because practising love and kindness is an embrace for all of life and all living systems. The belief that there is a choice between you and the planet is an illusion. Love and kindness are the ultimate global strategy, too. Use your awareness and your choosing to move out of the turbulence and join the flow.

Care

For many years, initially almost by accident, I have spent a portion of time with Anthroposophists – the people who are inspired by the philosophies of Rudolf Steiner. Anthroposophy is a spiritual philosophy and a spiritual science that seeks to understand the human being and their relationship with the universe. That seems to be a description of what I have spent my life doing and what this book is about.

I have been involved with two aspects of what he inspired. It started with education, born from the need for a school for my son that would support him to be the person he is. Waldorf education aims to do that. At its best it creates a context for children to experience the world for themselves. My second involvement has been with an organisation that has its roots in the Camphill movement, which created living communities to provide care and education, and subsequently adult living support, for people with special educational needs. I am happy to have been involved for twenty years with a local Special Education school and college. Though it is no longer a live-in community, it excels by upholding the value of creating an environment in which caring for the young people is delivered through care for everyone. Love and kindness are not merely an attitude. They are a practice that mirrors the development of the young person, of the carer/teacher and of the community. All grow and rise together.

Finding Peace

Last year, I joined my local Quaker meeting. Similarly, one attraction of Quakerism is its emphasis on the practice of love and kindness. It is what they do. They create a different kind of community. Their meetings, well-known for sitting in collective silent engagement with the Divine, are among the few places where one can regularly be among people who are practising together the kind of direct relationship with spirit that I am describing, without any prescription for what that consists of, or having any form of priesthood. People can be who they are and believe what they believe.

I introduce them here though, because while the movement has also inspired such work as prison reform and ethical business, the thing that Quakers are best known for is their focus on peace. For 400 years they have been stridently against war, foremost among conscientious objectors and those who refuse under any circumstances to kill others. They practice peace.

That doesn't mean that they have any simple solutions for the world's problems. For the context of this book, and for this concluding section about strategies for living and high vibration, it feels essential to explore, however briefly, how peace fits into that. It is one thing to have a spiritual aspiration and to raise one's consciousness. It is something else to make a difference in the day-to-day world.

I don't have any instant solutions either to generational conflicts, such as those in the Middle East. I only want to put peace into the context of what I have said about the requirement that the universe has for self-balancing. Family constellations exemplified the way in which that which is hidden, unresolved and out of balance in the Field of the family will continue to resonate through subsequent generations. Many of the healing modalities touched upon are similarly about the balances of spirit, embodiment and mind in what expresses physically.[45]

Achieving peace will also require balance. Peace is not the absence of war. Peace cannot be present when one group of humans are subjugating another group. It cannot be present when injustice is not addressed. Love and kindness, and their practical expression as care, become the means by which we seek the dynamic balance that is fundamental to Divine law. By nature the Information Field is open, but that openness is only theory unless and until we are in

---

[45] See the resources section for Gabor Maté's book "The Myth of Normality" which presents the many advances that have been made in conventional research that may eventually penetrate medical training and practice.

active relation to it. Balance is only achieved when we are all engaged in resolving issues in the field itself as well as by negotiating political settlements. Peace too, requires coherence.

If my description of the Field and of our personal continuities in it – the journey of our soul through time – is anything like correct, then the balances I am talking about are both individual and collective. At some point, in some incarnation I am likely to have been abuser and abused, perpetrator and victim, wife and wife-beater. At the level of the soul, when I judge and condemn others, I judge and condemn myself. Judgement and punishment do not in themselves bring healing or restitution. That is the big difference between human law and Divine law.

Care for individuals, care for ourselves and care for the entirety of living systems are the way in which we express love and kindness. These are the realities of how we raise our vibration. On the way, we may dance ecstatically, create art, be consummate in our sporting activities, have the most blissful of sexual connection or be at one with the gardens we tend. These can all be expressions of our Divinity, all aspects of releasing every aspect of who we are. Spirit can be found and explored anywhere. All of life can take place in relationship with the flow of the Divine, if that is how we choose to be.

Embrace all of who you are

My primary intention with this book was to expand your awareness of how much has contributed to making you the person you are. Close second, its supplementary purpose has been to open up the possibilities for who you can become and show how that will benefit us all. What if you being you is an intrinsic contribution to the creation of a much more desirable future?

I hope that seeing more of the layers and influences that have shaped you has made you feel richer and given you an even deeper appreciation both for yourself and your life journey and for the extraordinary wealth of humanity as a whole. I hope that the potential that lies in direct engagement with the Field has become visible to you, and thus inspired you to live more in that way, to become a relational being.

In addition, I strongly desire that this book will inspire new journeys. However much you have explored, there is always more. My experience has been that every one of the subjects we have touched on has had a contribution to make, taking away a block, delivering a new solution, improving my health, adding to my joy or contentment and propelling my work.

I am convinced that I could not have had the career that I did if I had not been opening myself in these ways. I know with certainty that I would not have managed the challenges that life has thrown at me, would not have the relationships that I have or the level of mental, physical and emotional health that I do by any other means. I see continuing this engagement as key to holding back the aging process and to achieving the goals that I still have. Insha'Allah. For example, I am still too serious, too much of the time, to be as joyful as I would wish. All that is aside from my aspirations to contribute to our future and Gaia's recovery. I embrace all of that. I am grateful for it all. There is perfection, plus expansion and integration. I am a work in progress.

Belong wherever you are

I want no less for you, so this book was meant to do more than engage your curiosity. I would love for it to trigger your active desire to experience even greater expansion for yourself. Maybe there is one chapter that you intuitively felt might be of particular value for you now. I encourage you to follow through on that impulse and find out what is there. I have done no more than provide limited introductions to the various topics. The resources list is there to support you in going deeper. Of course, you may also find even more by using Google and AI if you ask the right questions and push beyond the mass of conventional explanations. Remember though, that some of what you are looking for is beyond the material realm and its data. AI may be limited by what is available to it, and in consequence, behind the game.

I have endorsed the growing belief that the Universe has its own transition agenda, but that is not separate from us, not independent of our own transition. Humans are the visible extension of the Earth's consciousness. We hold a special place in the Field because of the ways we can imagine and create. The spirit of that creation is made physically through our actions. The transition agenda is not a given; it's not a manifest destiny unless we make it so.

The more that you can embrace and own this richness of who you are and the more that you can bring that forward into your harmonised co-creation as an element of the flow, the better that manifestation can get. As Helen Keller said, "*Security is mostly a superstition. It does not exist in nature, nor do the children of men as a whole experience it. Avoiding danger is no safer in the long run than outright exposure. life is either a daring adventure or nothing at all.*"

I hope that you will join me in that adventure, and I bless your endeavours. Together, we can go far.

Jon Freeman

Salisbury, UK

November 2025

Resources

Most of the following are references to books. Behind most of them are teachers, practitioners, YouTube channels, webinars and podcasts by those authors and their students. I encourage you to explore, with the reminder that if you do not feel comfortable or resonant with anyone or any approach you encounter, trust your knowing and move on. It took me a while to learn not to surrender my own authority. I stayed too long with some things that didn't work for me, or past the point where they were adding value, even when many of them were good for friends.

Chapter 1 – Discovering the Field

Book - "The Silva Method by Jose Silva
https://www.amazon.co.uk/Silva-Mind-Control-Method-Revolutionary/dp/B09PFD256S

Online training obtainable from MindValley

Monitor www.jonfreeman.co.uk/offers for details of forthcoming trainings in intuition

Chapter 2 – Echoes of the past

For Family Constellations: Book "Love's hidden symmetry by Bert Hellinger
https://www.amazon.co.uk/s?k=bert+hellinger+loves+hidden+symmetry&crid=2BZ1R1UGUE

For Systemic and Organisational work: Book - "Invisible Dynamics" by Klaus P. Horn https://www.amazon.co.uk/Invisible-Dynamics-Systemic-Constellations-Organisations-ebook/dp/B07HKFZN5X

Individual personal sessions online using Family Constellations – email Juliana Freeman –
Juliana@julianafreeman.co.uk

Systemic Constellations – contact
jon@futureconsiderations.com **– practitioners available in many regions.**

Chapter 3 - Early Influences

Book – Dr. Thomas Verny, "The Secret Life of the Unborn Child".
https://www.amazon.co.uk/Secret-Life-Unborn-Child-controversial/dp/0751510033

Book – Dr. Gabor Maté, "The Myth of Normal"
https://www.amazon.co.uk/Myth-Normal-Illness-Healing-Culture/dp/1785042734

Book - Dr Michael Newton, "Journey of Souls"
https://www.amazon.co.uk/Journey-Souls-Studies-Between-Lives/dp/1567184855

Book – Caroline Myss, Ph.D, "Sacred Contracts"
https://www.amazon.co.uk/Sacred-Contracts-Awakening-Divine-Potential/dp/055381494X

Chapter 4 - Form and Structure

Book – Candace Pert, "Molecules of Emotion"
https://www.amazon.co.uk/Molecules-Emotion-Why-You-Feel/dp/0671033972

Book – Bruce Lipton, "The Biology of Belief"
https://www.amazon.co.uk/Biology-Belief-Unleashing-Consciousness-Miracles/dp/1401923127

Chapter 5 – Genetics: Form, Structure and Being

Book – Jahan Hamshehazadeh, "The Psilocybin Connection"
https://www.amazon.co.uk/Psilocybin-Connection-Psychedelics-Transformation-Consciousness/dp/1623176549

Book – Merlin Sheldrake, "Entangled Life"
https://www.amazon.co.uk/Entangled-Life-Worlds-Change-Futures/dp/B084T51RCY

Book – Dorothy Mclean, "To hear the Angels Sing"
https://www.amazon.co.uk/Hear-Angels-Sing-Odyssey-Co-Creation/dp/0936878010

Book – Machaelle Small Wright, "Behaving as if the God in All Life Mattered" https://www.amazon.co.uk/Behaving-God-All-Life-Mattered/dp/0927978245

Chapter 6 – Expanding into US

If you are interested to explore or even to engage with healing your own early experience, inner child work can be very valuable. This book is seminal
John Bradshaw, Homecoming: "Reclaiming and Championing Your Inner Child"
https://www.amazon.co.uk/Home-Coming-Reclaiming-Championing-Inner/dp/0749910542

Chapter 7 – What's Nature to You?

Relevant book resources are as in Chapter 5, and also in the footnotes.

Chapter 8 – How we develop

Audiobook – Don Beck introduction to Spiral Dynamics
https://www.amazon.co.uk/Spiral-Dynamics-Integral/dp/B002SPZP3W

The SD "Bible"- Don Beck and Christopher Cowan – also translated in several languages
https://www.amazon.co.uk/Spiral-Dynamics-Mastering-Values-Leadership/dp/1405133562

Book on parenting through a Spiral lens – Jon Freeman, 7-stage parenting, French translation also available
https://www.amazon.co.uk/7-stage-Parenting-childs-changing-needs-ebook/dp/B08RY14LKH

More information and resources available at
www.sdifoundation.com

Chapter 9 – Understanding Mindsets

See Chapter footnotes

Chapter 10 - Contexts

Book – Jon Freeman, "The Science of Possibility - Patterns of Connected Consciousness"
https://www.amazon.co.uk/Science-Possibility-Jon-Freeman/dp/0956010733

Chapter 11 - Connection

Book – Pam Gregory, "You Don't Believe in Astrology, Do You?"
https://www.amazon.co.uk/You-Dont-Really-Believe-Astrology-ebook/dp/B0759KGR92

Pam also has a YouTube channel

Multiple resources for Genekeys (Richard Rudd) including free profile and many books / audios
https://genekeys.com/

Book – Don Richard Riso, "The Wisdom of the Enneagram: The Complete Guide to Psychological and Spiritual Growth for the Nine Personality Types"
Seems to be a recommended foundation

Good organisation used by people I respect. www.aephoria.co.za

Chapter 12 – Models and Maps

No specific resources

Chapter 13 – Beliefs and Experiences

Book – Targ and Puthoff, "Mind-Reach: Scientists Look at Psychic Abilities"
https://www.amazon.co.uk/Mind-reach-Scientists-Psychic-Abilities-Consciousness/dp/1571744142

Explore "International Consciousness Research Laboratories (ICRL)", successor to the PEAR labs (Princeton Engineering Anomalies Research). https://galileocommission.org/international-consciousness-research-laboratories/

This work has been subjected to the usual barrage of sceptical attack. Draw your own conclusions.

Book – J W Dunne, "An Experiment with Time" https://www.amazon.co.uk/Experiment-Time-J-W-Dunne/dp/B0BMKPKFWB

See also the footnotes and the resources for Chapter 1.

Chapter 14 – What could you know?

Book – Howard Gardner, "Frames of Mind: The Theory of Multiple Intelligences" https://www.amazon.co.uk/Frames-Mind-Theory-Multiple-Intelligences/dp/000686290X

Book and Audiobook – Cindy Wigglesworth, "SQ21, The Twenty-One Skills of Spiritual Intelligence" https://www.amazon.co.uk/SQ21-Twenty-One-Skills-Spiritual-Intelligence/dp/159079298X

Spiral Dynamics resources as above (Chapter 8)

Chapter 15 – Different ways of seeing

Relevant to the passage on trauma, and with much to say about embodiment and the entire holism of mind-body relationship, Gabor Maté's book is a significant complementary resource to this text, and a brilliant read/listen.

Book – Gabor Maté, "The Myth of Normal: Trauma, Illness and Healing in a Toxic Culture" https://www.amazon.co.uk/s?k=GAbor+Mate+myth+of+normal&i=stripbooks&crid=3US8WH766O5HF

Chapter 16 – Who can you be now?

I recommend investigating the work of Iain McGilchrist. His book "The Master and His Emissary" is brilliant. It is also very long, and more detailed. A simple 12-minute introductory lecture is available here https://youtu.be/dFs9WO2B8uI

He is a regular interviewee and there is an abundance of material on his own channel https://channelmcgilchrist.com/home/ This includes a rentable film "The Divided Brain"

Chapter 17 to 19 – Becoming, The Future of WE, The Ultimate Strategy

There are no specific materials for study here.

I am a long-time fan of the work of Caroline Myss, who is one of the deepest explorers and a most brilliant teacher about much of the world presented in this book. I know of no-one who has a more pragmatic sense of our relationship with the Divine. She can be challenging, though.

https://myss.com

Otherwise, it is an essential feature of this book's approach to assume that you may already know more in many areas than I do and that your path is unique. I am not necessarily the best guide for you and I encourage you to follow your instincts and intuition in that respect.

That said, I invite you to visit my website, www.jonfreeman.co.uk and to join the club of RB explorers. There will be both free and paid membership opportunities for our journey together. These days I am more motivated towards facilitation of collective expansion than I am towards individual coaching, though that remains available, for now.

I also invite you to follow me on Substack, relationalbeing.substack.com, where I write on topics that are often beyond the scope of this book. Included on the website is the work I do with organisations. This book has been very much oriented towards who we are individually and from within. At the same time, the Relational Being context has a lot to say about what happens when we come together. I still work as a consultant/mentor, where my background and experience with organisations and groups combine with both Relational Being and Spiral Dynamics in a potent approach to Organisational Development, optimising their existence by expanding their power as a living, intelligent system.

A note about other contributors.

Juliana Freeman is a remarkable human being, psychically aware as a child, extensively trained during her twenties in exploring the additional senses, both embodied and intuitive, and a continual explorer ever since. My own journey and the development of the ideas both in this book and in "The Science of Possibility" have been deeply informed and shaped by our explorations together. However much the books are my intellectual construction, and while she cannot be held accountable for anything in this one except where explicitly attributed, she and now Yvonne continue to contribute to my existence. I also recommend her strongly as a personal spiritual guide and multi-faceted connector to so many of the unseen realms, and as a family constellations practitioner. She and Yvonne are also guides for groups who wish to deepen their connections to sacred sites through engagement with the elemental forces.

Her electronic presence is limited, but you can contact her on https://www.linkedin.com/in/lifealchemy333/
Most of her work is offered remotely, but she is based, as described in the text, near the Malvern hills.

Dr. Steven Williams is the man who sorted out the torn ligaments in my shoulder after a year or more of failed treatments elsewhere. That happened almost 20 years ago and he has been helping me to maintain my structural health, and more, ever since, with just four short visits per year. As mentioned in the text, he is a world expert on paediatrics, and he is also a widely read investigator of other health support, such as nutrition and supplementation. His use of kinesiology, as well as his own intuitive understanding, are part of a whole-person, whole-body approach to treatment. He is an example of what is possible when a systemic approach is brought to bear, and of the mindset which this book is encouraging you to develop.

His practice is St. James' Chiropractic in Southampton, UK.

Modalities

I would like to give a sense of what the multi-layered depth of your existence means. What follows is an incomplete list of the ways in which I have explored this territory. They are not in any order – either time or importance. Some I trained in, some merely experienced. Nor are they equal in regard to the amount of engagement I gave them, but most delivered some value at the time. Often, issues that are stuck in one area can be released by another. In my experience, shifting between embodiment, mind, emotional and "energy"

I am certainly not telling you that you need any of them, still less all, and some I engaged in a long time ago are no longer available or are now outmoded. I did some things which don't have names and you may notice some surprising gaps, too, which indicate personal preference but not disapproval. If I had known then what I know now, I would probably have taken up yoga, chi gong or tai chi decades ago. But this is all by way of illustrating the complexity of our human systems, and what we might manage better, particularly if we were educated from childhood. Much of what I am describing has been rectification. If people were attuned to their bodies and responsive to their intuitive knowing our world would be very different.

Thus I am strongly suggesting that you can't discover all that is within you, and can't bring about change merely by thinking about it. Even after several decades, I still find that my life, health, growth and development benefit from a few that I still use, some that are new, and most of all, from always being willing to explore new things. I also believe it works physiologically. I am assessed as biologically a decade younger than my chronological age, have never had flu, rarely get colds for more than 2 days. Nothing is guaranteed, and perhaps I am not physically immortal, but so far, so good. ☺

The List

Re-evaluation co-counselling

Rebirthing / Holotropic breathwork

The Silva Method

The Loving Relationships Training

Colour-light therapy

Homeopathy

Acupuncture

Cranial Osteopathy

Osteopathy

Chiropractic

Reiki

Inner Child work

Past life work

Neuro-Linguistic Programming and Holistic NLP

Emotional Freedom Technique

Rolfing

Massage

Tantra (which for the avoidance of doubt, is not primarily about sex)

Channelling

Constellations – Family and Systemic

Spiral Dynamics

Enneagram, Myers-Briggs and other assessments

Astrology

Genekeys and Human Design

Access Consciousness (particularly Bars)

Five Rhythms dancing

Bio-Tuning

The Healy / Timewaver

Exercise – stretching, strength and aerobic. None of which I do enough of, and I wish I had started stretching much earlier.

Acknowledgements and Thanks

I hope you are reading these after the book so that what I say next makes sense.

Given the canvas of existence I have painted on here, it would not be inappropriate to acknowledge every person, conversation, book musician, film-maker etc. in my life, and even beyond. Nothing that I have written here comes from me. It all arises from that myriad of relationships. It is an original piece of work assembled from borrowed scraps onto structures mostly created by others.

I also know that I have been guided spiritually by other beings, some of whom have names that are only meaningful to me and some of whom are nameless. More tangibly I have been supported by events and synchronicities. Even though I can sometimes be anxious and fearful about the realities of my life, I have found that the Universe has my back. Ultimately, this book intends to encourage you that we can all live that way.

Amidst all of that, there are of course individuals who deserve mention here, including a number who were not knowingly involved because they have been part of conversations that stimulated my thinking, prepared the background and shaped some of what I said, including by disagreement. These include my colleagues in Future Considerations Ltd and many in the Spiral Dynamics community, and the SDi Foundation, notably Auke van Nimwegen, Rasa Kvaukeite, Rica Viljoen, Michael Keller, Ben Levi, Marilyn Hamilton, Annelies Weijschede, Petra Pieterse.

For their more direct involvement I name the following. Bianca Clarke who has brilliantly shaped my website and is orchestrating my communications. Marcos Frangos for some early conversations about Relational Being, which include the recordings you can find on my YouTube channel. Various readers who coped with the early draft and made helpful comments: Edwina Forshaw-Gumbrill, Kurt Christiansen, Ralph Rickenbach, Rhian Morallee, Shereen Mohd Idris. Jeannet Weurman for recent conversations. Peter Thomson, sales, marketing and communications genius, for advice on the title, even if I ignored much of it.   As all authors rightly say, none of these people bears any responsibility for my eventual choices.

To anyone who deserved a mention and didn't receive it, I offer my apologies.   To all of you, and to all of life, I am profoundly grateful.